MEDITATIONS FROM
Mechthild
of Magdeburg

Edited and Mildly Modernized by
HENRY L. CARRIGAN, JR.

PARACLETE PRESS
Brewster, Massachusetts

Library of Congress Cataloging-in-Publication Data

Mechthild, of Magdeburg, ca. 1212-ca. 1282.
    [Fliessende Licht der Gottheit. English. Selections]
    Meditations from Mechthild of Magdeburg / edited and
mildly modernized by Henry L. Carrigan, Jr.
        p.   cm.
    ISBN 1-55725-217-3 (pbk.)
    1. Visions—Early works to 1800. 2. Private revelations—
Early works to 1800. 3. Spiritual life—Catholic Church—
Early works to 1800. 4. Meditations. I. Carrigan, Henry L.,
1954-   . II. Title

BV5091.V6M43413 1999
248.2'2—dc21   99-11222
                                                    CIP

10 9 8 7 6 5 4 3 2 1

Published by Paraclete Press
Brewster, Massachusetts
www.paraclete-press.com

Printed in the United States of America.

Contents

Introduction

BIOGRAPHY

There are no biographies of Mechthild by her contemporaries. Almost everything we know about Mechthild's life, work, and writings comes from her principal book, *The Flowing Light of the Godhead*.

Mechthild was born to noble parents sometime between 1207 and 1210 somewhere in the archdiocese of Magdeburg, in Germany. Although we know nothing about her parents, the numerous references in her writing to the Court and its language and custom indicate her noble birth. Mechthild had one brother, Baldwin, whom we learn, from *Flowing Light* (FL), became a Dominican. According to the Latin version of FL IV. 26, "Brother Baldwin, blood brother of Sister Mechthild, was brought up in childhood in good manners and was instructed in all virtues. He was steeped in scholastic training. Because of the merits of his sister, he was received into the Order of Preachers, where he made such progress in virtue and knowledge that his brothers promoted him to the office of subprior." Mechthild's description of her brother also lends credence to the theory of Mechthild's nobility.

As a child, she tells us, she was a "simple spiritual creature." She says that she "knew nothing of God except the

usual Christian beliefs," and she tried to follow those diligently. Before her religious revelation, Mechthild acknowledges she strove to be "despised through no fault of my
own." She also writes that before she received the Holy
Spirit's outpouring, she "knew nothing of the devil's
wickedness, the veil of the world," or the hypocrisy of religious people.

She reports that when she was twelve years old, she was
"greeted" by the Holy Spirit so that "she could no longer
give in to serious daily sin." This outpouring of the Holy
Spirit continued daily in Mechthild's life, she says, for the
next thirty-one years, and it brought her love and sorrow
and sweetness and glory.

Sometime between 1230 and 1233, when she was twenty-
three, Mechthild left her home and moved to Magdeburg,
where she knew only one person. But she avoided this
friend, because she was afraid that "because of this friend
my renunciation of the world and my love of God might be
hindered." (IV.2) In Magdeburg, she joined the Beguines.

The Beguines were a lay women's religious movement
that flourished in the thirteenth century. According to one
scholar, "they did not follow any established rule, but lived
lives of apostolic poverty and chastity doing works of char-
ity among the poor and the sick."[1] The Beguines strove to
live a spiritual life in the midst of the world, and their religious lives were marked by fervent prayer, asceticism, and
ardent devotion to the sacraments. The Beguine movement produced four of the greatest medieval mystics:
Beatrijs of Nazareth, Hadewijch, Gertrude of Helfta, and
Mechthild of Magdeburg.

Mechthild's own experience with God was congenial
with Beguine spirituality. She describes her first experi-

---

[1]   [Saskia Murk-Jansen, *Brides in the Desert: The spirituality of the Beguines.*
Maryknoll: Orbis, 1998, p. 12]

ence with God: "He brought me such sweetness of love, such heavenly knowledge, such inconceivable wonders, that I had little use for earthly things. Then I saw the beautiful figure of our Lord Jesus Christ with the eyes of my soul." (IV.2) Her description of Christ as a beautiful youth permeates Mechthild's writing. Most often, she casts herself as a bride who is waiting for this beautiful young Bridegroom to penetrate her with His love and suffering.

Sometime around 1250, she began to write the book we now have as *The Flowing Light of the Godhead.* After many years of "painfully conquering her body" and enduring illnesses because of her asceticism, Mechthild reports a conversation with God in which He commands her to write down her experiences with Him. God tells Mechthild He will take care of her physical and spiritual needs as she undertakes this task. When Mechthild goes to her confessor, the Dominican Heinrich Halle, he tells her to "go forward with great joy and write this book out of God's heart and God's mouth." (IV.2) Although she tells us that she feels unworthy to undertake such a task, for the next fifteen years or so Mechthild writes down on loose papers her revelations, visions, and conversations with God. Various scholars differ on just what sections of *Flowing Light* Mechthild produced during these years. While some think that she had completed Books I–VI by 1260, others think that she wrote Books I–V between 1250 and 1260 and that she wrote Books VI and VII much later. Some also contend that Halle circulated the first six books during Mechthild's lifetime.

Mechthild remained in Magdeburg for many years, most likely living in the Convent of St. Agnes. She might have been the Superior at this convent sometime between 1265 and 1273, and her writings about the duties of a Superior (VI.1) indicate she could have held such a position. However, Mechthild's life in Magdeburg became increasingly difficult.

She openly denounced the abuses of the medieval Church, particularly its materialism. For a time she was barred from Communion and her Daily Offices, and many labeled her writings heretical. Even within her own community, many considered her ideals too lofty to be practical. Thus, Mechthild left Magdeburg sometime between 1270 and 1285.

Mechthild sought refuge in the Cistercian convent at Helfta, where Gertrude of Hackeborn (1250–1291), a woman of great piety and intellect, was abbess. The convent at Helfta was a center of intellectual activity and spiritual enrichment. In addition to Gertrude's encouragement of study and copying of manuscripts, Helfta was home to two great medieval visionaries, Mechthild of Hackeborn, whose visions were written down in *The Book of Special Grace,* and Gertrude of Helfta, who wrote an account of her own spiritual life in *The Herald of Divine Love.* Such an atmosphere both intimidated and encouraged Mechthild. Due to a long illness soon after she came to Helfta, though, Mechthild became blind, and she had to dictate her writings, including Book VII of *Flowing Light,* to the nuns. She died in Helfta sometime between 1282 and 1297.

MEDITATIONS

The meditations collected in the present book are drawn from Mechthild's *The Flowing Light of the Godhead.* I have not reproduced the entire book here, but have selected those sections that address most directly the spiritual life. I have not included, for example, those sections in which Mechthild focuses on the regulations of the convent or admonishes or counsels specific nuns within her community about their own spiritual problems.

I hope readers can use these meditations as guides in their own spiritual lives. Mechthild often depicts the relationship between the seeker and God as the relationship between bride and Bridegroom. Using the exalted and lyrical language of the biblical Song of Songs, Mechthild often describes the intimacy between Christ and the contemplative in erotic terms. More than that, just as she seeks to lay her restless heart in God's heart, so her poetic meditations encourage contemplatives to place their restless hearts in God's heart.

The great theme of Mechthild's book is Divine Love. Like Augustine, who reminds his readers that God is "the love with which the soul loves You," Mechthild believes that God's great Love is the Source of all things, most especially the soul's love. Consequently, the soul longs to return to its Source. Mechthild provides glimpses of the soul's journey to God. It first strips away all earthly pleasures, then ascends to Christ, and eventually ascends to God and His love, where God and the soul mingle like water and wine. Mechthild describes this journey: "The rippling tide of love that all her life had flowed secretly from God into her soul drew it back mightily into its Source." (VII.45)

Mechthild's sparkling, crystalline poetry and her golden prose dazzle its readers and hearers with God's majesty and God's grace. Although she acknowledges her lowliness in approaching God, Mechthild convinces all contemplative seekers that God's grace enables us to soar to God's heavenly heights, if only we are open to receive it.

A WORD ABOUT THE TEXT

The text of *The Flowing Light of the Godhead* I have used here comes from *Revelations of Mechthild of Magdeburg*, London: Longmans, Green, and Co., 1953. There are no chapter titles in this edition, for Mechthild's original edition lacks specific chapter titles. Rather, I have followed Mechthild's structure and the chapters here are called "Books." In addition, I have numbered the meditations in each Book consecutively for easier reading. For accuracy's sake, however,

I have placed Mechthild's original numbering system in parentheses following the new numbers. Thus, in Book I, meditation 7 appears as "7 (13)," since this is meditation 13 in Mechthild's text.

I have remained true to the spirit of the text, even where I have mildly modernized it. Mostly, my modernizations have come in three areas. First, I have replaced archaic words and forms of address with more modern ones. Thus, "Thou" becomes "You" throughout. Second, I have attempted to use inclusive language in this edition. I have retained the masculine pronouns for God, so as not to be anachronistic. But, wherever Mechthild speaks of "man," in a generic fashion, I have used "humanity" instead. I have also replaced the third person masculine pronoun, "he, his, him," with the third person feminine pronoun, "she, hers, her," when the referent is a generic word like sinner, for though Mechthild uses the masculine, she is always referring to herself. Finally, I have altered the syntax and sentence structure of the writing to make it livelier and more appealing to a contemporary audience. Most often this simply means casting sentences in the active rather than the passive voice.

I trust and pray that Mechthild's meditations will inspire and exalt your soul as they have mine.

Henry L. Carrigan, Jr.
Westerville, Ohio

Prologue

ALL SEEKERS SHOULD WELCOME THESE MEDITATIONS joyfully, for God speaks through them. I send them as a message to all spiritual people, both the good and the bad. With great praise, the meditations proclaim God's holiness. Everyone who hopes to understand them should read them nine times.

"O, Lord God, who wrote these meditations?"

"I wrote them in my powerlessness, because I did not want to hide the gift that is in it."

"What should these meditations on your great Glory be called then?"

"They should be called the flowing light of my Godhead into all hearts free of hypocrisy."

BOOK
I

1. A Dialogue Between Love and the Soul, Who is the Queen

SOUL: "God greet you, Lady Love."

LOVE: "May God reward you, O Queen."

SOUL: "O Love, I am pleased to meet you."

LOVE: "I am honored by your greeting and admiration."

SOUL: "Many years did you struggle with the Holy Trinity, O Love, until you convinced the Holy Spirit to pour itself into Mary's virginal womb."

LOVE: "I did all these things for your delight and your honor."

SOUL: "Lady Love, you have taken from me everything I have gained on this earth."

LOVE: "It is a quite happy exchange, my Queen."

SOUL: "But you have taken my childhood from me."

LOVE: "Only in exchange for heavenly freedom, my Queen."

SOUL: "You have taken my youth from me."

LOVE: "Only in exchange for many virtues."

SOUL: "Lady Love, you have taken from me all my friends, my relatives, my honor, and my possessions."

LOVE: "With the presence of the Holy Spirit, I shall make up to you as many of these losses as you wish in one hour's time, my Queen."

SOUL: "O Love, you have made me endure such trial and suffering that I am barely alive."

LOVE: "But, my Queen, in the place of that loss you have gained great understanding."

SOUL: "O Love, you have devoured my very flesh and blood."

LOVE: "Because of this loss, you are enlightened and raised up to God."

SOUL: "Love, you are a thief; You must repay me for all my losses."

LOVE: "I will repay you, my Queen. I beg you, take me."

SOUL: "You have paid me back many times over, O Love."

LOVE: "Now you possess God and all His heavenly realm, my Queen."

2. Concerning Three Persons and Three Gifts

God's true greeting, flowing out of the Trinity, has such great power that it takes the strength from the body and reveals the soul to itself, so that the souls sees itself as one of God's blessed ones and dresses itself in divine radiance. Separating itself from the body, the soul flies toward God with power, love, and longing. Such a little bit of life is left in the body, it feels as though it is plunged in a sweet sleep. The soul then sees God as One and Undivided in Three Persons, and Three Persons as one Undivided God.

God greets the soul in His heavenly language. He clothes the soul with heavenly garments, and gives the soul strength, for whatever the soul asks, God will grant it.

God and the soul soar to a blissful place, and the Infinite God brings the soul up into the heights of contemplation. In the face of such wonder and splendor, the soul loses touch with the earth and forgets it was ever upon the earth. Yet, when it reaches the highest point of its flight, the soul must abandon its flight.

Then the All-Glorious God speaks: "O Soul, you must become humble and return to earth and your body."

Frightened, the soul cries out to God: "O Lord, You have brought me up to such Glory that I will find it difficult to praise You when I return to my body, for I will struggle ceaselessly against the longings of my body."

God replies: "My dove! Your voice is music to my ears; your words are spices for my mouth; your longings are beautiful gifts."

The soul says: "Lord, I will do as You command."

With a deep sigh, the soul awakens the body, and the body asks: "Soul, where have you been? You've returned to me so lovely, free, and full of spirit, but you have taken all my power, energy, and peace from me."

The soul cries out: "Be quiet! Quit complaining! I will always be on guard against your ways. I am not upset to hear that you are hurt; I am glad for it."

O, fiery and radiant God, now that You have given me, the least of your servants, a taste of your sweet Glory, I am hungry for the taste of the rich glory You have given the greatest of your servants. I will happily suffer here even longer so that I may have that experience."

3. The Handmaids of the Soul and the Blow of Love

SOUL: "Dear Love, how long have you been lying here waiting for me? What can I do? You have hunted, captured, and bound me, and you have wounded me with blows of such force that I will never heal or recover from you. Wouldn't it have been better if I had never known you?"

LOVE: "I hunted you for my pleasure, and for my desire I caught you. For my joy, I bound you. Your wounds have made us one. I chased Almighty God out of Heaven, and I took His human life and gave Him back again with honor to His Father. Poor worm, how could you hope to escape me?"

SOUL: "Lady Love, I fear a small gift God has often given me so I might prosper in your presence."

LOVE: "As one gives prisoners bread and water so they will not die, God has given you this small gift, a respite for a time. But, when death comes to you, when your Easter comes, I will be around you and through you, and steal your body and give you to your Love."

SOUL: "Dear Love, I have written these words for you; seal those words with your sign."

LOVE: "The one who loves God more than herself knows where to find the seal; it lies between the two of us."

SOUL: "Be silent, dear one, and speak no more. Dearest of all maidens, let all creatures, myself included, bow down before you. Tell my Lover that His bed is made ready, and that I am weak with longing for Him."

4. *The Soul's Journey to the Court, During Which God Reveals Himself*

The impoverished soul comes modestly and cautiously to Court, and she looks at God with joyful eyes. She is lovingly received there. The soul is silent but longs above everything to praise Him, and He wants to show her His Divine heart, which is warm and glowing. God places the soul in His glowing heart so that He, the great God, and she, the humble mind, are united as one. She is overcome with weakness, and He is overpowered with love for her. Then, the soul exclaims: "Lord! You are my Beloved. My desire. My flowing stream. My Sun. And I am Your reflection."

5. Of the Torment and Reward of Hell

My body is tormented, and my soul is exceedingly delighted, for she has seen and embraced her Beloved. Through Him, she suffers torment. As He draws her to Himself, she gives herself to Him. She cannot hold back, and so he takes her to Himself. She is engulfed in union with the glorious Trinity. He gives her a brief respite so she may long for Him. She desires to praise Him, but she cannot. She prefers He send her to Hell, if only all creatures might love Him above all things. She looks at Him and says, "Lord! Give me Your blessing!" He draws her to Him and greets her as the body cannot greet her.

Thus the body says to the soul: "Where have you been? I can't bear this anymore."

The soul replies: "Silence, you fool! I will remain with my Love, even if you don't get over it. I am His joy, and He is my torment." This is my torment, which I will always endure and never escape.

6. Concerning the Nine Choirs and How They Sing

Listen, my love, and hear with spiritual ears the music sung by the nine Choirs:

We praise You, O Lord:
> You have sought us in Your humility,
> You have saved us by Your compassion,
> You have honored us in Your humiliation;
> You have led us by Your gentleness,
> You have ordered us by Your reason,
> You have protected us by Your power,
> You have sanctified us by Your holiness,
> You have illumined us by Your intimacy,
> You have elevated us by Your love.

7. (13.) How God Comes to the Soul

I come to My love as dew comes on the flowers.

8. (14.) How the Soul Receives and Praises God

Ah, joyful sight!
Ah, lovely greeting!
Ah, loving embrace!
Your Glory has crushed me and Your Mercy has overwhelmed me. O You mighty Rock, You are so nicely riven that you provide rest for doves and nightingales.

9. (15.) How God Receives the Soul

Welcome, sweet dove!
You have flown so long over the earth
That your wings are strong enough to lift you up to
Heaven!

10. (16.) How God Compares the Soul to Four Things

You are as sweet as the grape.
You are as fragrant as balsam.
You are as radiant as the sun.
You are an enhancement of My highest love!

11. (17.) The Soul Praises God in Five Things

O God! You are so generous in pouring out
    Your gifts!
You are so flowing in Your love!
You are burning in Your desire!
You are fervent in Your union with Your beloved!
You who rest on my heart,
Without You I can no longer live!

12. (18.) God Compares the Soul to Five Things

O you beautiful rose among the thorns!
O you fluttering bee in the honey!
O you unblemished dove in your being!
O you beautiful sun in your radiance!
O you full moon in the firmament!
I cannot turn away from you.

13. (19.) God Caresses the Soul in Six Things

You are my resting-place, my love, my secret peace, my
deepest longing, and my highest honor. You are a delight of
my Godhead, a comfort of my manhood, and a cooling
stream for my ardor.

14. (20.) The Soul Praises God in Six Things

You are a mirror of my vision, my eyes' delight, an escape
from my self, my heart's tempest, a fall and a weakening of
my power; yet, You are my highest security.

15. (21.) Of Knowledge and Revelation

Love without knowledge
Is darkness to the wise soul.
Knowledge without revelation
Is like the pain of Hell.
Revelation without death
Cannot be endured.

16. (23.) Pray That God Love You Often and Long, So You Shall Become Pure and Beautiful and Holy

Ah, Lord, love me passionately, love me often, love me long. For the more continuously You love me, the purer I will be; the more fervently You love me, the more beautiful I will be; the longer You love me, the holier I will become here on earth.

17. (24.) How God Answers the Soul

Because I Myself am Love, I will love you
    continuously.
Because I long to be loved passionately, My desire is
    to love you fervently.
Because I am everlasting and eternal, I will love you
    long.

18. (25.) How to Bear Suffering Gladly for God

God guides His followers in mysterious ways. God Himself walked in a mysterious, noble, and holy way: for the One without sin and guilt suffered pain. The soul who longs for God rejoices in the nature of its Lord who through His great goodness endured much suffering. For the Father gave His beloved Son to be tormented by unbelievers and to be martyred in spite of His sinlessness. In these days, many people who appear to be spiritual torture God's children in body and torment them in soul, because God wills that His followers should be tormented in body and soul as His Son was so tormented.

19. (26.) In This Way the Soul Leads the Senses and Is Free and Without Grief

The faithful soul walks in a wonderful and lofty way, leading the senses after it as a person with sight might lead a blind person. In this way the soul is free and travels without grief, for it wills nothing but what the Lord wills, and He does everything for the best.

20. (27.) How You Are to Become Worthy of the Way, Walk in It, and Be Perfected

There are three things that make the soul worthy of this Way, so it recognizes the path and walks in it. First, it renounces all self-will, joyfully welcoming God's grace and accepting grace's demands rather than human desires. Second, the soul welcomes all things except sin. Third, the soul does all things to God's glory, so God will honor the soul's smallest desire as if it were the highest state of contemplation.

The soul does everything in love to God's glory; thus, all is one. But, if I sin, I am no longer in this way.

21. (28.) Love Shall Endure Until Death, Without Measure and Without Ceasing

I rejoice that I love the One Who loves me, and I pray that I may love Him without measure and without ceasing until the day I die. Rejoice, O my soul! for He gave His life because of His love for you. Love Him so deeply that you would gladly die because of your love for Him. In this way you will burn as an inextinguishable spark in the fire of the living Majesty:

> So you will be filled
> With Love's Fire,
>   Therefore you are happy here!
> You don't need to teach me any more
> For I can never turn away from Love;
> I am Love's prisoner,
> Otherwise I could not live.
> Where Love lives I will live,
> In death also as in life.
> (Life without sorrow
>   Is the folly of fools.)

22. (29.) Of the Bridegroom's Beauty and How the Bride Should Follow Him

Look at Me, My Bride, and see how beautiful My eyes are! Look at My elegant mouth! See how delicate My hands are and how My heart burns with fire! See how swift My feet fly! Now, follow Me!

You will be martyred with Me. You will be betrayed because of envy, tempted in the desert, imprisoned because others hate you and Me, and denounced by the slanderous. Your eyes will be covered so you cannot recognize the truth. The anger of the world will beat you down, and You will be brought to judgment, beaten with sticks, crowned with temptation, and spit upon with contempt. You will bear your cross because you hate sin, and be crucified because you have renounced all things by your own will. You will be nailed on the cross by the holy virtues, wounded though love, and you will die on the cross in holy constancy. Your heart will be pierced by constant union, and you will be taken down from the cross, victorious over your enemies. You will be buried in humility, raised from the dead to blessedness, and drawn to Heaven by God's breath.

23. (31.) You Should Not Pay Attention to Contempt

I was despised by many. Then our Lord said: "Don't be surprised! If people cruelly despised the precious container of the Chrism, what could happen to the container of vinegar, which contains nothing good in itself?"

24. (32.) You Should Not Pay Attention to Honor or Sorrow, But You Should Avoid Sin

If someone offers you honor, be ashamed. If you are tormented, rejoice! If anyone does good to you, be fearful. If you sin against Me, your heart should be full of sadness. If you cannot be sad, reflect upon how long and how deeply I was saddened for you.

25. (33.) Of the Trust and Love of a Beneficiary

My soul thus spoke to her Love: "Lord! Your tenderness is wonderful gift to my body, Your compassion is a great comfort to my soul. Your love is eternal rest to my entire being."

26. (34.) In Suffering You Will Be as a Lamb, a Dove, and a Bride

You are My lamb in your sufferings,
My dove in your sighings,
And My bride in your waiting.

27. (35.) The Desert Has Twelve Things

You shall love nothingness,
You shall flee the self.
You shall stand alone,
Seeking help from no one,
So your being may be quiet,
And not bound by any thing.
You shall give liberty to the captives,
And encourage those who are free.
You shall care for the sick,
Even though you dwell alone.
You shall drink the waters of sorrow,
And kindle love's fire
With the kindling of virtue—
This is the way you shall live in the desert.

28. (36.) Of Malice, Goodness, and Wonders

You shall be adorned with the malice of your enemies.
You shall be honored with the virtues of your heart.
You shall be crowned with your good works.
You shall be raised up because of our mutual love.
You shall be sanctified with My glorious wonders.

29. (37.) The Soul Replies That She is Not Worthy of Such Graces

Beloved! I am delighted by undeserved contempt;
I desire the virtues of the heart,
Alas! I have no good works,
I tarnish the beauty of our two-fold love,
And I am unworthy of Your glorious wonders!

30. (38.) God Rejoices That the Soul Has Overcome Four Sins

Our Lord is happy in Heaven
Because of the loving soul He has on earth,
And He says, "Look how the soul who has wounded
Me has risen!
She has cast away from her the apes of worldliness.
She has overcome the bear of impurity,
And she has trampled the lion of pride,
And torn lust and desire from the wolf's mouth.
She comes panting like a hunted deer
To the spring, which is Myself.
She comes soaring like an eagle
Flying from the depths
Up into the heights."

31-35. (39-43.) God Asks the Soul What It Brings

GOD: What do you bring Me, My Queen?

SOUL: Lord, I bring You my precious treasure;
It is greater than the mountains,
Wider than the world,
Deeper than the sea,
Higher than the clouds,
More glorious than the sun,
More numerous than the stars,
It outweighs the entire earth!

GOD: O you, the image of My Divine Likeness,
Made noble by My humanity,
Adorned by My Holy Spirit,
What do you call this precious treasure?

SOUL: O Lord, I call it my heart's desire!
I have kept it away from worldly things,
I have denied others and myself my heart's desire.
Now I can no longer carry it.
Where, O Lord, shall I lay it?

GOD: You shall place your heart's desire nowhere
But in My own Divine Heart
And on My human breast.
There alone you will find comfort
And My Spirit will embrace you.

36. (44.) Of Love's Way in Seven Things, Of Three Bridal Robes, and Of the Dance

GOD: Loving soul! Would you like Me to show you the path you should follow?

SOUL: Yes, Holy Spirit, show it to me.

HOLY SPIRIT: You must move beyond the need for remorse, the pain of penance, the weary toil of confession, the love of the world, the temptations of the devil, the desires of the flesh, and the self-will, all of which hold the soul back from ever finding real love. When you have conquered these enemies, you will be weary and exclaim, "Beautiful Youth, where can I find you?"

YOUTH: I hear a voice
That speaks out of love.
I have pursued her for many days
But I have never heard her voice.
Now I am moved—
I must go to meet her,
For she carries grief and love combined.
In the morning dew is when the delightful intimacy
of inwardness
First penetrates the soul.

THE SENSES (who are the soul's chambermaids): Lady! You must adorn yourself!

SOUL: Ah, Love! Where shall I go?

THE SENSES: We have heard a whisper.
Do not dawdle,
For the Prince comes to greet you,
In the morning dew, while the birds are singing.

So, the soul dresses in a slip of humility, so humble that only her nakedness would be more humble. Over this slip, she wears a white dress of chastity so pure that she cannot bear any words or desires that might stain it. Next, she wraps herself in a cloak of Holy Desire woven from all the virtues.

Thus, she goes into the woods, the company of holy people. The sweetest nightingales sing there day and night, and she hears also the pure notes of birds singing of holy wisdom. But, the Youth does not come. He sends her

messengers, for she wishes to dance. He sends her
Abraham's faith, the Prophets' longings, the chaste mod-
esty of our Lady Saint Mary, our Lord Jesus Christ's sacred
perfection, and the entire company of His elect. So a noble
Dance of Praise is prepared. Then the Youth comes and
speaks to her: "You shall dance merrily, even as one of My
elect!"

SOUL: I cannot dance, O Lord, unless You lead me.
    If it is Your will that I leap joyfully
    You must first dance and sing!
    Then I will leap for love,
    From love to knowledge,
    From knowledge to consummation,
    From consummation beyond all human sense.
    There I will remain
    And circle evermore.

YOUTH: You have performed well your Dance of Praise.
    Now, the Virgin's Son will grant you your desires.
    You are weary! Come at noon
    To the shade by the brook,
    To love's resting-place.
    There you will be able to cool yourself.

SOUL: Ah, Lord! It is too much
    That You should be my companion in love
    Since the heart has no love in itself,
    Unless that love is aroused by You.

Wearied by the dance, the soul says to the senses:
"Leave me alone! I must rest myself." The senses reply to
the soul: "Lady, will you be refreshed sufficiently by Mary
Magdalene's tears?"

SOUL: Be quiet, for you do not understand me.
    Leave me alone for a few minutes so I can drink of
    the pure wine.

SENSES: Lady, God's love is ready for you in virgin chastity.

SOUL: Even so, this is not the highest path for me.

SENSES: Why don't you cool yourself in the blood of the
  martyrs?

SOUL: I've been martyred so many days that the path is no
  longer sufficient.

SENSES: Many pure souls abide by the counsel of their con-
  fessors.

SOUL: I will obey their counsel, but I will not follow that
  path.

SENSES: Surely you can find solace in the wisdom of the
  Apostles?

SOUL: I have their wisdom in my heart, and it leads me to
  choose the better part.

SENSES: Lady, the angels are clear and bright and full of
  Love.

  Ascend to them if you want to cool yourself.

SOUL: Unless I see my Lord, my Love,

  The angels' joy is sadness to me.

SENSES: Refresh yourself in the holy austerity God gave to
  John the Baptist.

SOUL: Pain and suffering are not sufficient, for Love rules
  over all.

SENSES: Ah, Lady, if you want to be refreshed,

  Look at the Child on the Virgin's lap

  And taste and see how the angels drink of Eternity

  In the Virgin's milk.

SOUL: To suckle and cradle a baby is childish love.

  I am a full-grown Bride,

  And I want to go to my Lover's side.

SENSES: Ah, Lady, if you go directly there,

  We will be blinded,

  For the glory of the Godhead burns so bright

  That all the flame and all fires' glow

  In Heaven and on earth below

  Flow directly out of God's Divine lips

And from the counsel of the Holy Spirit.
Who can stand such fire, even for one hour?

SOUL: Fish cannot drown in the water,
Birds cannot sink in the air,
Gold cannot perish in the refiner's fire.
God has given all creatures the desire
To seek and foster their own nature,
How then can I resist?
  I must go to God—
My Father through nature,
My Brother through humanity,
My Bridegroom through love,
I am His forever!
Do you think fire will kill my soul?
No, Love can fiercely scorch
As well as tenderly love and comfort.
Therefore, don't be troubled.
You shall continue to teach me when I return,
For I will need your teaching
Since the earth is full of snares.

Then the beloved goes in to the Lover, into the secret
hiding place of the sinless Godhead. There, since the soul
is fashioned in the likeness of God, no obstacle can come
between God and the soul.

LORD: Stand, O Soul!

SOUL: What is Your will, Lord?

LORD: Your self must leave.

SOUL: But Lord, what will happen to me then?

LORD: By nature, you already belong to Me,
Nothing can come between us.
There is not even a heavenly angel
Who is granted for one hour
What you are given forever.
Thus, put away all fear and shame and all outward
  things.

Only the things of which you are sensible by nature
Shall you want to be sensible in Eternity.
This shall be your noble longing and endless desire.
In My infinite mercy, I will forever fulfill this desire.

SOUL: Lord, now I am a naked soul
And You are a Glorious God.
Our mutual intercourse is Love Eternal
Which can never die.

Now comes a blessed stillness
That both welcome. He gives Himself to her
And she gives herself to Him.
The soul knows what is going to happen to her.
Therefore, I am comforted.

Dear friend of God, I have written down this path of love
for you. May God place it in your heart. Amen.

37. (46.) Of the Bride's Many Ornaments

The Bride is clothed with the sun and treads the moon
under her feet. She is crowned with union. She has a chap-
lain whose name is Fear. He has a golden rod in his hand,
that is Wisdom, and Wisdom is clothed with delight and
crowned by Eternity.

The Bride has a beast of burden: the body. It is bridled
by unworthiness and fed on contempt. Its stable is confession. The pack it carries is innocence. The Bride has a purple silk cloak; it is hope, adorned with truth and crowned by
song. She has a palm in one hand—forgiveness of sin, and in
the other hand she has a box filled with desire and love.
These she takes to her Lover. Her hat of peacock's feathers
denotes holiness on earth and high honor in Heaven. She
follows the path of meekness, adorned with inclination and
crowned with certainty. As she goes, she sings:

Ah, chosen Love, I long for You!
You love me but give me a heavy heart.
The need I suffer for You is not of this world!
Whenever You command it, Lord,
Then only shall I be released from the self.

BRIDEGROOM: O love most worthy of My love! Remember
    the hour
When you first recognized My full demand
And you feared you had power to ever attain it.
Yet, I waited for you and I held you in My arms!

THUS OUR LORD SAID TO HIS CHOSEN BRIDE: Come, My
    Beloved, come. You shall be crowned.

Then He gives her a crown of truth that only spiritual
souls may wear. In the crown one sees four virtues, Wisdom
and Sorrow, Desire and Discipline. May God give us all this
crown! Amen.

BOOK II

1. Love Raises the Soul but Not the Senses, for Self-Will Comes from the Senses

The soul reaches its heights in love, while the body reaches its heights in Christian baptism. There is nothing higher than love, and Christianity is elevated in glory. Those who try to climb to these heights of love simply by their own efforts greatly deceive themselves, for they do not possess the virtue of holy humility which alone can lead the soul to God. Once self-will has gained control of the heart, false holiness creeps into the heart.

2. Of Two Love Songs

I would die of love willingly if this happened to me.
I have seen Him Whom I love within my soul.
The bride who provides a place for her Lover
No longer needs to seek Him.
Love does not easily go away
When young girls seek their lover:
His noble nature is always ready
Eagerly to welcome His bride
And draw her to His heart.
Those who are unwilling to seek Love
May easily miss this.

3. (5.) A Song of the Soul to God: How God is the Garment of the Soul and the Soul a Garment of God

You shine in my soul
As the sun shines on gold.
When I rest in You, O Lord,
My happiness is overwhelming.
You clothe Yourself with my soul;
You Yourself are its cloak.
If the two had to be separated
I would have greater sorrow than any I have ever
   suffered.
If You want to love me more
Then I must journey to that place where I will be
   able to love You without ceasing.
Now I have sung to You,
Yet without success,
If You would sing to me,
Then I would surely succeed.

4.(6.) God's Reply to the Soul in Five Things

When I shine, you will reflect my radiance,
When I flow, you will flow swiftly,
When you breathe, you draw into yourself My
Divine Heart.
When you cry for Me, I take you into My arms.
When you love Me, we are united as one.
Nothing can separate us, for we abide together
   joyfully.
Then, O Lord, I will wait for You with hunger and

thirst, eagerness and delight
Until that joyful hour when the chosen words flow
from Your lips.
Only the soul that cuts itself off from the world
to listen to the words of Your mouth will hear
them.
Such a soul alone is able to receive the Fount of
Love.

5 (7.) Of Praising God in Sorrow; Of Two Golden Chalices: Sorrow and Consolation

When I, a sinner, went one day to my prayer, it seemed that God would listen to me or extend me His Grace. I lamented my human frailty, which was a great obstacle to me in my spiritual life. But my soul said: "Think instead of God's faithfulness and praise Him for it. Glory to God in the highest!"

When I praised God in this way, a great light appeared to my soul. God, in all His great glory and unspeakable clarity, was Himself in the light. Our Lord lifted up two golden chalices in His hands, and both were full of living wine. The chalice in His left hand was filled with the red wine of suffering, and the one in his right hand was filled with the white wine of precious consolation. Our Lord said: "Blessed are the ones who drink this wine. Even though I offer both in Divine Love, the white wine is nobler in itself. But, most blessed are those who drink both the white and the red."

6. (8.) Of Purgatory; How One Person Releases a Thousand Souls with Tears of Love

A certain person prayed very earnestly, yet simply, to God for suffering souls.

God showed her Purgatory's terrible cleansing fire,

And the many sinners whose torments were equal to the number of their sins.

Her spirit was so moved by such suffering that she seized all Purgatory in her arms.

She endured all the suffering, but asked Love to help her.

Then God spoke: "Do not hurt yourself by carrying a burden too heavy for you."

Her spirit replied sadly: "Lord, I pray that You will set some free."

He said: "How many would you like Me to free?"

She said: "As many of those for whom, by Your Mercy, I may make atonement."

Our Lord said: "Take a thousand souls."

Then the poor creatures raised themselves out of Purgatory, and they were burned, bleeding, and dirty. The spirit spoke: "Lord, what will happen to these creatures now? For they cannot enter Your Kingdom in this awful state." Then in His mercy God spoke a comforting word: "You shall bathe them in the tears of love that flow from your eyes."

All at once they saw a great basin. The unhappy beings dove into it and bathed in Love as bright as the sun. The spirit felt inexpressible joy and said: "All creatures will praise You for ever. Now these are fit to enter Your kingdom." Our Lord bent down from on high and placed on their heads the crown of Love which had redeemed them and said: "You shall wear this crown forever so all in My Kingdom will know that you have been released by tears of love nine years before your proper time."

7.(9.) God Praises His Bride in Five Things

You are a light of the world.
You are a crown of virginity.
You are a healing ointment for all wounds.
You are faithfulness in the midst of falsehood.
You are a bride of the Holy Trinity.

8. (10.) The Bride Replies, Praising God in Five Things

You are the Light in all lights.
You are a flower lovelier than all crowns.
You are a healing salve for every illness.
You are unchangeable truth without falsehood.
You are a host in every inn.

9. (11.) Of God's Sevenfold Love

True love of God has seven forms:
Joyful love walks in God's path,
Bashful love accepts labor,
Strong love is eager to do great things,
Loving love does not seek fame,
Wise love has knowledge,
Free love lives without the heart's sorrow,
Powerful love is joyful forever.

10. (12.) Of Sevenfold Perfection

To be eager to be dishonored, to be eager to be neglected, to be eager to be alone, to be eager to be quiet, to be eager to be lowly, to be eager to be esteemed, to be eager to be one among many.

11. (13.) There Shall Be Love Between God and the Soul

Between you and God there shall be love forever;
Between you and earthly things there shall be
    uneasiness and fear;
Between you and sin there shall be hatred and strife;
Between you and the Kingdom of Heaven there shall
    be everlasting hope.

12. (14.) The Causes of Various Things

Bitterness of heart comes from human frailty;
Weakness of the body comes from the flesh;
A lively spirit comes from nobility of soul;
Fear of suffering comes from a guilty conscience;
The body's illness comes from nature;
Need and misery come from pride;
To be rarely joyous comes from restlessness of spirit.

13. (15.) How a Soul Wounded by Love is Healed

Whoever is grievously wounded by love will never become whole unless she embraces the love that wounded her.

14. (17.) How God Frees the Soul and Makes It Wise in His Love

In this way God frees the simple soul and makes it wise in His love. Ah, sweet dove, your feet are red, your wings are smooth, your eyes are beautiful, your travels are happy, your flight is swift; but all too soon you return to the earth.

15. (18.) How the Soul Touches the Freedom of God in Eight Things

Lord, my feet are spotted by the blood of Your Redemption. My wings are smooth because You have nobly chosen me. My mouth is directed by Your Holy Spirit, and my eyes are illumined by Your fiery Light. My flight is hastened by Your unresting care. I sink to earth because of Your union with my body. The greater release from earthly things that You give me, the longer I will soar in You.

16. (19.) How Understanding and the Soul Speak Together

UNDERSTANDING: Loving soul, I have been watching you as
     you are wondrously wrapped in your love.
I was given a light so I could see this, for otherwise I
     could not have seen it.
You yourself are triune
So you are in God's likeness.
Though you battle your strife like a male warrior,
You are richly adorned like a young virginal woman
In your Lord's palace,
A happy bride in the resting-place of love.
God-loving soul, in your struggles

You are armed with measureless strength and with
such great power of soul

That all the world's peoples, all your body's charm,
all the devil's legions,

And all the powers of Hell,

Cannot separate you from God.

You arm yourself as with flowers,

Your sword is the glorious rose, Jesus Christ,

And, thus, you protect yourself.

Your shield is the white lily, the Virgin Mary,

She adorns you and increases in you God's immea-
surable glory.

God's Majesty will richly reward all who engage in
this warfare.

Ah, noble soul, what is your position in the palace of your
Holy Trinity, where you stand so beautifully adorned by
your Lord?

SOUL: Understanding! Why do you ask me? You are wiser
than I am.

UNDERSTANDING: Because, O Soul, you are my Mistress and
Queen, and God has chosen you above all things.

SOUL: Understanding, I was born with nobility and freedom.
I may not go without honor, for I love God alone. I
must, therefore, win God's love, caresses, and honor.

Then the Holy Trinity and all Heaven and earth will
be subject to me.

If I let Love control me and bind me in holy patience,
so I do not increase my sin,

It will lead me to a noble gentleness and will prepare
me for good things.

It will make me obedient and lovingly subject to God.

UNDERSTANDING: Ah, Bride, if you could only give me a
glimpse of the unspeakable intimacy between you
and God.

SOUL: I cannot do so, for no bride may tell what happens to
her.

You might hear of holy revelations and pleasures
from me,

But God's supernatural teachings must be hidden
from all except me alone.

UNDERSTANDING: Soul, if you will simply reveal a tiny
glimpse of the miracles and lofty words

You have seen and heard in God,

Then I could provide a royal light for a dark and
foul-smelling stall.

SOUL: But the cattle are content to eat straw.

If some, who only appear to be God's children,

Rustle about like cattle in a dark stall and speak of
things about which they know nothing,

They do so only from pride and hypocrisy.

One reads that St. Paul was taken up to the third
Heaven.

If he had remained Saul, or found the truth in the
first or second Heaven,

He would never have ascended to the third!

The devil makes a heaven with his false cunning.

There thought wanders in sad reflection

And the soul suffers silently,

For it doesn't find what it wants.

There the soul remains uncomforted and betrays the
simple senses.

In this heaven the devil appears as a glowing angel
similar to God even in the five wounds.

Simple soul, beware!

The second Heaven is formed from the senses' holy
longings and from love's first part.

In this heaven there is no light, and the soul does not
see God there.

But the soul is conscious of an unspeakable sweet-
ness flooding through its entire being.
It also hears a voice speaking about many of the
things it eagerly desires,
For its life is still entangled with earthly things.
If the soul does not have deep humility,
The devil brings his light, and what happens then is
not of God.
But, if true humility is there,
The soul may journey forth to the third Heaven,
For there it is given its true light.

THE SENSES: Lady, your soul has been asleep since childhood;
Now the light of true love wakens it.
In this light the soul looks around to discover herself
And to see who reveals Himself to her.
Now she clearly recognizes how God is all in all.
Now I lay aside my anxieties and cares
And journey with St. Paul to the third Heaven,
If in His love God will cast away my sinful body.
The third Heaven is vaulted and ordered and illu-
minated by the Three Persons.

17. (22.) Contemplation Asks the Soul about the Seraphim and the Lowest Human Beings

CONTEMPLATION: O Soul, would you rather be a heavenly
seraphim or a human being with body and soul in
the lowest choir of angels?

SOUL: You have seen, Contemplation, how the seraphim
are noble princes that are one love, one fire, one
breath, and one light with God.

CONTEMPLATION: But surely, Soul, you have seen that angels
are simple beings that can praise and love and recognize God according to their capacities. Even the

lowest human being can be like the angels through repentance, longing, and good will, although her soul may not burn so fervently in the Godhead.

SOUL: You have surely seen, Contemplation, that the seraphim are God's children and still His servants.

The smallest soul is the daughter of the Father, the sister of the Son, the friend of the Holy Spirit, and truly the Bride of the Holy Trinity.

Let us see which creature weighs heaviest upon the scales.

Jesus Christ is the worthiest of all angels; He soars above the seraphim,

And is One Undivided God with the Father.

Yet I, the least of all souls,

Take Him in my hand and eat Him and drink Him and do with Him what I will.

That can never happen to the angels, however high above me they are.

His Godhead is never so unreachable that I cease to be aware of Him in all my being.

Thus, my ardent love of Him can never cool.

Why, then, should I be concerned about what the angels experience?

18. (23.) *How Love Questions and Teaches a Dull Soul and Would Gladly Bring It to Its Love*

LOVE: Where are you, foolish soul?
Where and how do you live?
Where can you find any rest
If you won't place the God who rejoices in you
Above your own powers and your own will?

SOUL: Leave me alone! Since I am not awake to you,

I don't understand what you're saying.

LOVE: One must wake up the Queen
When her King wants to come to her.

SOUL: I belong to a holy Order.
I fast, I watch, I am without mortal sin.
I am sufficiently bound to God.

LOVE: What use is it to fix an empty barrel if the wine still
flows out?
Then one must fill it with the stones of outward works
And the ashes of the past.

SOUL: I live in the joy of companionship and the company
of good spiritual friends.
How can I deeply love Him Whom I don't know?

LOVE: Don't you know the Lord whose name has been so
lovingly spoken to you?
You are more interested in the pleasures of the body
than in your sweet Lord Jesus.
You can win little honor in His eyes.

SOUL: I live according to my own will
Which I hope to bring to perfection.

LOVE: If you perform true service to God,
You must follow His Holy Spirit in love.

SOUL: I take comfort in the world of my body.

LOVE: Before God, you should be ashamed.
How dare you speak of spiritual things
Yet welcome only the pleasures of the body.

SOUL: But how can I support myself if I must burden
myself with you?

LOVE: You're so unfaithful! He who made the soul so noble
that it can enjoy nothing but God will never
allow the body to lack anything.

SOUL: You reprimand me very severely.
If I only knew where He was,
I might still turn to Him.

LOVE: If you want to live with him in noble freedom,

You must first clear your heart of evil habits.

SOUL: Alas, few can do that.

Those who are wise through learning or common sense

Dare not put themselves in the power of pure love.

LOVE: But God naturally turns to the pure in heart who honor only God in all they do.

SOUL: If I had turned to God, might I have risen very high?

LOVE: What use is it to put beautiful clothes on a sleeping person, or to place fine food in front of her?

She will not want to eat the food.

Beloved, let me wake you up.

SOUL: Tell me then where I can find His dwelling.

LOVE: There is no lord in the world

Who lives in all His dwellings at once,

Except for God.

He lives in the peace of holy love and whispers with His love.

In the narrow confines of the soul,

He embraces her in the noble pleasure of His love.

He greets her with His loving eyes,

And when they gaze on each other in truth,

He kisses her with His Divine lips.

He courts her powerfully with His grace,

She comes to the highest blessedness,

And the sweet sorrow of love is in her very soul.

SOUL: O Love, don't arm yourself with anger.

Who are the ones who arm themselves like this?

LOVE: They are the ones who bother themselves and others with evil.

Now, I will tell you who God is:

He is higher than the Highest

And yet has lowered Himself to the lowest valley,

And the lowest valley has set itself up on the highest heights.

Foolish soul, open your eyes and take a look at yourself.

SOUL: If He has come down from the highest heights because He loves me,

And He has given Himself with all His creatures entirely to me,

Then I am eternally ashamed,

For I never exchanged my worthless copper for His precious gold.

Where have I been? Unblessed, I have been blind and have lived so long

Without that powerful love by which I might have overcome my need.

Though I have failed to do much good,

I will now give up all earthly things for God.

Love, will you still receive me?

LOVE: Yes, God does not deny Himself to anyone.

But, that counts both ways:

If you want to have love, you must leave love.

19. (25.) The Complaint of the Loving Soul When God Appears to Shun It and Withdraw His Gifts; How the Soul Asks God Who and What It Is; Of a Garden of Flowers and of the Singing of Maidens

O countless and abundant treasure! O infinite and incomprehensible Wonder! O endless honor in the Majesty of Your Glory! How bitter it is when You shun me.

Even if all creatures lament for me,

Not one could tell You fully

What inhuman need I suffer.

Death would be far gentler to me.

I seek You in my thoughts as a bride seeks her groom.
When I am bound to You I suffer grievously, for the bond
is stronger than I am,
And I can never free myself from Love.
I call You with deep desire and mournful voice.
I wait for You with a heavy heart.
I cannot rest, and I burn without pause in Your flaming
love.
I seek You with all my strength.
Love, don't run so fast and so far ahead
But rest a little so I may catch up with you.
Lord, since You have taken all I had of You, give me Your
grace. I desire this more fervently than Your heavenly
Kingdom.

"Sweet dove, listen to Me.
My Divine Wisdom soars so far above you
That I have to arrange My gifts to you, or else you could
not bear them in your poor body.
Your loving pursuit has made me so weary that I long to
refresh Myself
In your pure soul where I am imprisoned.
The throbbing sighs of your suffering heart have driven
My justice away from you.
This is well, for I cannot be cut off from you.
We cannot be separated no matter how far apart we are.
I cause you bitter pain no matter how lightly I touch you.
If I were to give Myself to you as often as you desired
I would deprive Myself of the dear refuge I find in you
in this world.
For even a thousand beings could not contain a loving
soul's desire.
The higher the love, the more blessed the pain."

"Lord, You spare my dark prison where I drink the
    world's sorrows and eat with misery
The ashy bread of my human lacks
And am wounded by the fiery rays of Your love.
Now leave me here, O Lord,
Unanointed and in my torment."

"My Queen, how long will you be impatient?
If I wound you grievously, don't I also heal you lovingly at
    the same time?
My Kingdom's greatness is all yours, and you shall have
    power over Me Myself.
I lovingly bend toward you always.
All you have done and lost and suffered for Me
I will give to you again,
And I will grant you eternal forgiveness for everything
    you desire."

"Lord, teach me two things in Your mercy:
If my lips are silent because of my simple understanding,
If my tongue is full of laments,
If my senses ask me hourly what is wrong with me,
All this You have given me, Lord.
If my flesh falls away from my bones and my blood
    evaporates,
If my limbs dry up and cramps torment my blood vessels,
If my heart melts in Your love,
If my soul burns like a hungry lion's roar,
Tell me, Beloved, where will You be then?
How shall I fare?"

"You are just like a new bride
Whose lover, to whom she has given herself trustingly,
    has left her sleeping.
She cannot endure even one hour of his absence.

When she wakes up and finds herself alone, she laments
    bitterly,
For it is more than she can bear.
But, even while the youth is not by her side, his Bride is
    always with him.
He says: 'I come to you at My pleasure; you must be
    modest and quiet.
If you will just hide your grief, your love will grow
    stronger.
Now, I will tell you where I will be:
I am in Myself, in all places, all things,
As I always have been, without beginning.
I wait for you in the garden of love
I pick for you the flower of sweet union,
I make a bed of love in the pleasant meadow of Holy
    Understanding.
The bright sun of My Eternal Godhead shall shine on
    you
With the hidden wonder of My love that you have
    secretly generated in Me.
You shall pick the green and white and red apples of My
    gentle humanity from the highest branch
Of My Holy Trinity.
The power of My Holy Spirit shall protect you so lov-
    ingly from all earthly sorrow that you will
No longer feel such sorrow.
Once you embrace the tree
I will teach the song of the young virgins.
Even some of them, who are still troubled by desire, may
    not yet understand the way, the words,
Or the sweet melody of this song.
Come, love! Sing on and let Me hear
How well you can sing this song.'"

"Alas, my Beloved, my throat is dry because of my
   innocence.
But Your sweet gentleness brings back the music to my
   voice
So I can now sing this song:
Lord, Your blood and mine are one, unstained.
Your love and mine are one, undivided.
Your robe and mine are one, unspotted.
Your lips and mine are one, unkissed."

Such are the words of love's song:
May the heart's sweet music remain in it forever,
For no earthly pen could ever write it!

20. (26.) Of This Book and Its Writer

Many warned me about this book and told me I should
not preserve it but burn it. When told this, I did what since
childhood I have done when I have faced trouble: I began
to pray. I bowed myself to Love and said:
   "Lord, I am troubled: Must I walk uncomforted for Your
      Glory?
   You have misled me, for You Yourself commanded me to
      write."
   Then God revealed Himself to my weary soul, and, hold-
      ing the book in His right hand, He said:
   "Beloved, don't worry too grievously.
   No person may burn the Truth.
   Those who would take this book from My hand must be
      stronger than I!
   This book is threefold and concerns Me alone.
   The parchment before Me deals with My pure, right-
      eous and wise humanity
   That suffered death for you.

The words describe My glorious Divinity which flows
hourly from My Divine Mouth into your soul.

The voice of the words signifies My Living Spirit and
fulfills in itself the living Truth.

Now, see how all these words gloriously proclaim My
holiness.

Do not doubt yourself."

"Lord, if I were a learned priest and You had worked this
wonder in me, You would receive endless honor.

But how can anyone believe that You could build this
golden house, where Your mother, all creatures, and all
the heavenly host reside, on such unworthy soil?

In that, God, I can see no earthly wisdom."

"Daughter, many wise people lose their precious gold
carelessly on the great highway they must travel to Me.

But someone must find it!

For a long time I have acted in this way:

I looked for the lowest and smallest and most hidden
whenever I gave special grace.

The highest mountains may not receive revelations of
My Grace,

For the flood of My Holy Spirit flows by nature down
into the valleys.

One finds many a writer of wise books who is, in My
sight, a fool.

Furthermore, I am greatly honored and the Holy Church
powerfully strengthened

When unlearned lips teach learned tongues of My Holy
Spirit."

"Lord, I sigh and long and pray for Your scribe,
Who copied this book for me.

Reward him with grace never granted to man.

For Your Grace, O Lord, is a thousand times more powerful than Your creatures can ever receive."

Then Our Lord spoke:

"He has written it in letters of gold.

Thus, he shall inscribe every word of it on his cloak in gleaming, heavenly gold:

For pure love must always be the highest of all human attributes."

When the Lord said these words to me, I saw the glorious Truth in eternal merit:

Lord, I pray You will preserve this book from the eyes of the false, who are conceived in Lucifer's heart, born in spiritual pride, reared in hatred, and grown up in scorn without virtue.

God's children must suffer from this and be oppressed by such infamy if they follow Jesus and receive God's highest honor.

We must always watch ourselves and our fellow Christians with loving care,

So, if they should err, we may warn them faithfully and save ourselves many unnecessary words.

BOOK
III

1. (2.) How The Soul Praises God in Seven Things and How God Commands Her to Wait Patiently for Healing

Sweet Jesus, unconcealed from my poor soul's love and need, I praise You in love, in need, and in fellowship with all creatures. To praise You delights me above everything else. Lord, You are the sun of all eyes, the joy of all ears, the voice of all words, the power of all courage, the teacher of all wisdom, the love in all life, and the order in all being.

Then, with His great pleasure, God praised the loving soul: "You are a light before My eyes, a lyre to My ears, a voice for My words, a meaning for My joy, an honor of My wisdom, a love in My life, a praise in My being."

SOUL: Lord, You are eternally wounded because of Your love for me.

You have proved this well.

You have written me in the book of Your Godhead,
You have fashioned me in Your own image,
You have bound me hand and foot to Your side.
Let me anoint You, Beloved.

GOD: But where will you find the ointment, dear heart?

SOUL: Lord, I will tear my heart in two and place You there.

GOD: You could never give Me a more precious gift than to soar ceaselessly in your soul.

SOUL: Lord, as long as I abide in You, I will be Your physician.

GOD: Yes, I will allow you to be My physician.

But My faithfulness to you means you must wait quietly.

My love commands you to work,
My patience commands you to keep silence,
My concern commands you to bear poverty,
My longing commands you to endure contempt,
My desire commands you to endure need,
My conquest commands you to pursue all virtues,
My end commands you to bear much—
> In all this you have honor until I can take your heavy burden from you.

2. (3.) A Complaint That the Soul is a Servant and of God's Love

SOUL: Lord, what a poor and neglected soul is the servant of Your love here on earth. Who can help me express the soul's suffering, for she does not understand what she lacks.

LOVE: But, O Bride, don't you say in your book of Love that Love runs away from you? How can that be? I would rather die of pure love than let God escape from me because of my lack of knowledge. When I am able to take pleasure in my Love, then wisdom can teach me nothing. But when I have to work at other things with my five senses, I rejoice when I receive the holy Mass. Listen, dear friend, I was joyful because I was drunk with Love and thus spoke tenderly of the five senses. When I have drunk too deeply of Love, I can no longer think of my Love, for I must do whatever Love commands and wills. I must adjust myself to what God desires, for if He takes my body, my soul belongs to Him as well:

> If you come with me to the tavern, it will cost you a great deal.

Even if you had a thousand dollars, you would spend
it all in one hour.

If you want to drink the undiluted wine, you must
always spend more than you have,

And the host will never fill your glass to its brim!

You will become poor and naked, and be despised by
those who will not offer their all in the cellar.

The friends who go with you to the inn will also look
at you with contempt.

They will scorn you because they dare not pay such
a great cost for undiluted wine,

But they must have water mixed with wine.

Dear Bride, I would gladly spend all I have in the
tavern,

I would let myself be dragged through the fires of
love so I may often make my way

To the heavenly inn.

SOUL: I do not want to lose Love, either. He despises and
torments, yet he pours for me the Host's own wine
that He Himself has drunk.

I am so intoxicated with this wine that I am truly
subject to all creatures,

And it seems to me that in my sin and dishonor no
greater evil could be done to me.

Thus, I do not seek revenge on my enemies, even
though I know they would gladly break God's
commandments to harm me.

LOVE: Dear Friend, when the inn closes and you must go
out into the street poor, hungry, naked, and so
despised you no longer have any support of
Christian life except faith alone, then if you will
love, you shall never suffer ruin:

Bride, I have such hunger for the heavenly Father,

That I forget all sorrow.

I have such thirst for the Son that it takes away all

my earthly desire.

I have such need of the Spirit of both that it transcends all I can grasp

Of the Father's wisdom,

Of all the Son's work I can bear,

And of all the comfort of the Holy Spirit that may come to me.

Whoever has such need must always have an undeserving dependence on God's holiness.

3. (4.) *How Our Lady Could Sin and How Not, As the Holy Spirit Teaches This*

Mary, Mother of God. Someone asked me whether or not you could sin like other human beings, because you lived on this sinful earth. The Holy Spirit, who knows all things, has taught me how you could have sinned. God created you a complete human being and did not lay aside your human attributes. Thus your purity and nobility were precious in God's sight.

But, divinely noble as you were above all human beings, you could not sin. You didn't have it in you, for the heavenly Father, with the forethought of His choice, protected you as a child. The Holy Spirit surrounded your youth with His new love, and Jesus passed through your body, as dew through the flowers, so that you remained a pure virgin. The power of the Holy Trinity bound your nature so that it could never wish to sin against its Creator. The eternal wisdom of the Godhead overshadowed you so that the facts of human life were revealed to you, so you would suffer pain without sin, and so your humanity would not be lost, even though you bore the Son of the Almighty Godhead.

Even in these shadows, you humanly carried Jesus and nurtured him as his mother. But, the Word of the Son, the fire of the Godhead, the light of the Holy Spirit, and the wisdom of the Son were so great in you that you could hardly find rest. God knows how you then must have had to struggle with poverty and adversity. But, in your heart you remained fervently committed to the good work, inspired by the great Fire that burns in itself without beginning and without substance. That fire, O Lady, illuminated your being and drove all shadows out of your home.

4. (5.) How the Soul Laments That It Cannot Hear Mass Nor the Daily Offices; How It Praises God in Ten Things

A sorrowful soul complained that God had cast her aside from His great love and loved her by means of great suffering. Alas, how grievously those who have been rich can suffer once they fall into poverty. The soul exclaimed: "Lord, I am now so poor in my sick body, so exiled in my soul, and so deprived of spiritual privileges that no one reads Your Offices to me or celebrates the Holy Sacrament of the Mass for me."

Thus spoke the Lord's voice of love:
It pierced my soul with His great words
And I was unworthy to hear them:
"You are my desire; My love thirsts for you.
You are a refreshing presence in My breast,
You are a powerful kiss to My mouth,
You are a great joy to My being!
I am in you and you are in Me.
We two could not be closer,
For we are united as one,
Poured into one mould,
Thus, unwearied we shall remain forever."

Lord, You speak as if You were right here beside me. Yet, I dare not think too joyfully of Your words, for my body always stinks and my enemies attack me constantly. But, I know nothing of sorrow when I contemplate You, for You have taken me from myself and hidden Yourself in me. Our Lord answered:

"I must teach you My deepest searchings, My furthest wanderings, My highest desires, and My hopeful expectations. For noble young virgins must pay dearly for their training; they must conquer themselves in all their sufferings and many times tremble before their disciplinarian.

That is the lot of My brides on earth. I was once on earth because of My great love for you. I bore mockery and poverty for your sake, and My enemies taunted Me with My death. Still, I trusted in My Father's unspeakable goodness. Fashion your courage according to that pattern!"

5. (6.) If You Would Rightly Follow God You Must Have Six Things

Whoever would follow God in honest works must keep moving. She must reflect upon herself as a sinner and upon herself now as virtuous. She must lament and praise and pray day and night. When a faithful bride wakes up, she thinks of her love; if she cannot be with him, she weeps. How often this happens spiritually to God's brides.

6. (7.) Of Seven Enemies of Our Bliss Who Do Us Sevenfold Harm

To be useless is a bad habit, and bad habits harm us in every way. Earthly desire destroys God's holy word in us, and the hard struggle against pride greatly injures us.

Discord of heart drives the Holy Spirit from us. Angry passions take us from our intimacy with God. False holiness can never endure while pure love of God never passes away. If we do not conquer these enemies, they will take more than Heaven from us, for if we are holy we can have a foretaste of Heaven even here on earth. But, if we allow these enemies to conquer us, they will rob us of the seven gifts of the Holy Spirit and extinguish in us God's light of true love. They also cover the eyes of holy knowledge and lead us blindly into the seven deadly sins. And, where does that lead, if not into the eternal abyss?

7. (9.) Of the Beginning of All Things God Has Made

Father of all Good! I, an unworthy creature, thank You for all the faithfulness with which You have drawn me out of myself and shown me Your wonders. In Your undivided Trinity I heard and saw the glorious heavenly Council that ruled before Creation. At this time You, O Lord, were enclosed in Yourself alone and had no one to share in Your unspeakable joy.

Then the Three Persons shone so brightly in One

That each shone through the other and yet was complete in itself.

The Father was adorned in Omnipotence. The Son was like the Father in unspeakable Wisdom, and the Holy Spirit was like both in perfect gentleness.

Then the Holy Spirit spoke gently to the Father: "Lord and Father, I will give You some gentle counsel: We will no longer be alone. We will have a creative Kingdom and make angels that resemble Me and that are one spirit with me; the second spirit shall be humanity.

"For Joy alone is the great love and inconceivable

happiness we share with others in Your Presence."

Then the Father spoke: "You are one spirit with Me; whatever You advise pleases Me. When the angel was created, You know what happened. Even if the fall of the angel had been prevented, humanity still had to be created. The Holy Spirit gave the angels His goodness so they would serve us and take pleasure in our blessedness."

Then the everlasting Son spoke His mind: "Dear Father, My nature, too, must bear fruit. Since We are working wonders, fashion humanity after Me. Although I can see great trouble ahead, I must love humanity eternally."

Then the Father spoke: "Son, I, too, have a great longing in My Divine heart, and I hear the call of love. We will become fruitful so humanity will love Us in return and recognize Our great glory. I shall make Myself a Bride who shall greet Me with her mouth and wound Me with her glance. Then love will have its beginnings."

Then the Holy Spirit said: "Dear Father, I will lead Your Bride to You."

And the Son spoke: "Father, You know I have not yet died for love. Yet let Us begin these things in great joy and holiness."

Then the Holy Trinity created all things and made created humanity's body and soul. Adam and Eve were fashioned nobly after the pattern of the Everlasting Son, whom the Father generated without beginning. The Son shared His heavenly wisdom and His earthly form with Adam:

That he might have true knowledge and holy senses to offer to all earthly creatures in perfect love.

Then the Lord gave Adam a modest and noble young woman, Eve, to love. He gave her the same humble love He Himself had for His Father. Their bodies remained pure, for God did not create anything they would be ashamed of, and they were clothed like angels. They were to conceive their children in holy love. But, from the time

they ate the forbidden fruit, their bodies were altered so
that they did feel shame, as we still do today. If the Holy
Trinity had made us like angels, because of the noble
nature of that creation, we would have had no need to be
ashamed.

The heavenly Father shared His Divine love with the
soul and said: "I am the God of all gods; you are the god-
dess of all creatures and I give you My solemn vow that I
will never forsake you. You will not lose yourself, for My
angels will always serve you. I will give you My Holy Spirit
as your guardian so you will not fall mistakenly into mortal
sin. I also give you free will. You shall Love above all things
and you shall act always with prudence.

You shall keep a simple law
Which you must always remember:
I am Your God!
The soul that feeds on the pure food
God left for it in Paradise,
Shall remain in great holiness in its mortal body.
But, because Adam and Eve ate the food not intended
     for them
They lost angelic purity and forgot chastity.
Then for many years the soul called for her love with a
     sorrowful voice saying:
"Lord, when did Your sweet love come?
How grievously You have banished Your rightful Queen."
Then the Holy Trinity held a solemn council.
The Father spoke: I repent of My work
For I had given the Holy Trinity so noble a bride that the
     highest angels
Should have been her chambermaids;
If Lucifer had remained in his place of honor, she would
     have been his goddess.
For her alone I prepared the wedding bed
But she wished no longer to be like Me.

Now she is horribly misshapen, and who would accept such dirt?

The everlasting Son knelt before His Father and said: "Give me Your blessing. I will take her. I will gladly take blood-stained humanity upon Myself, heal its wounds with My innocent blood, and bind the wounds with the cloth of humility. Through human death I will make restitution to You for human sin."

Then the Holy Spirit spoke: "Almighty God, We will make a noble procession in glory down from these heights. I have already visited the Virgin Mary."

Then the Father consented in great love to Their wills and said to the Holy Spirit: "Carry My light before My dear Son into all those hearts He shall touch with My words. But You, Son, shall take up Your Cross. I will go with You in all Your ways and give You a pure young woman as a mother, so You may more nobly elevate low-minded humanity."

Then the procession moved joyfully into the Temple of Solomon where Almighty God took refuge for nine months.

8. (10.) The Passion the Loving Soul Has from God; How It Rises and Goes to Heaven

The longing soul sighing for God reveals her true love. She is sold in holy lamentation for her love. She cries many tears for her dear Lord whom she longs to find. She is captured when God kisses her in sweet union. She is seized by many holy thoughts as she humiliates the flesh so she will not waver in her love. She is bound by the Holy Spirit's power and her delight is infinite. She is so overwhelmed that she cannot bear the everlasting Light without resting. She is dragged trembling in shame before the Judge because God withdraws from her so often due to her sins. She answers all things modestly and would not willingly anger anyone. She is shouted at, beaten and grievously wounded, when she must return to her body. She is clothed with the purple of great love. She is crowned with infinite fidelity when she praises God with her faithfulness rather than asking Him to reward her for it. She is scoffed at because she loses herself so completely in God that she forgets earthly wisdom. Others mock her for kneeling at the feet of all creation. Her eyes are blinded by the unworthiness of her body where she lies imprisoned in darkness. She bears her cross along a pleasant way because in her suffering she gives herself to God. Because in her holiness she seems like a fool, people strike her. She is nailed so firmly to the cross by Almighty Love's hammer that no one can release her. She thirsts greatly on the cross of Love and she would willingly drink the pure wine of all God's children.

Then they all come and offer her bitter drink.
Her body is slain in living Love,
And her spirit is raised up above all human comprehension.
After this death she goes to Hell and comforts the sorrowing souls with her prayers of God's goodness,
Though her body does not feel it.
She is pierced in her side, and much holy teaching pours out of her heart.

She hangs high on the Cross of Love in the pure air of the Holy Spirit, turned toward God's Son and oblivious to all earthly things. When she is taken down from the cross, she says: "Father, take my spirit. It is finished." She is laid in a sealed grave of deep humility for she has always known that she is the most unworthy of creatures.

She rises happily on Easter Day, having joyfully talked with her Love during the night. In the early morning, with Mary Magdalene, she comforts her chambermaids when she is assured that God has blotted out her sins. Her body distresses her, for it would command her with its vulgar will. But she insists to the virtues: "I am your Mistress. You must obey me in all things. If I had not gone to the Father, you would always remain fools."

Then she ascends into Heaven where God takes all earthly things from her. She is received into a white cloud of holy protection where she is lovingly carried aloft and she returns free from all cares. Then the angels come and comfort the Man of Galilee, when we remember God's chosen friends and their holy example.

Every soul truly penetrated by God's love will endure such passion.

9. (12.) You Shall Praise, Give Thanks, Desire and Pray; Of the Light and the Lantern

Dear Lord, I was so poor that I could neither think of all these words, nor pray, nor love. Then I crept over to You and said: "How can I honor You now?" And You said to me, the most unworthy of all creatures: "You shall praise Me for My faithful protection, thank Me for My bountiful gifts, desire My holy miracles, and pray for a holy end." I write this in tears. May God help me, poor creature, remain always in Jesus. Then my Love spoke: "I will set a light in the lantern and a special ray of understanding shall illumine every eye that sees the light." Then the soul asked in great humility: "Beloved, what shall that lantern be?" Our Lord answered: "I am the Light. Your breast is the lantern."

10. (22.) Of God's Compassion, Temptation, and Righteousness

I have seen and heard of God's such boundless compassion that I asked: "Lord, how can that be?"

If Your righteousness accompanies Your compassion,

how can Your mercy be so great?

Then our Lord spoke:

"I tell you there are more in Holy Church who go
straight to Heaven than go down to Hell.

Even if it is stained by sin, righteousness has its own constant power.

For I come first of all as Father to the burdened soul.

If I have learned something good from the soul, it is the
temptation I endure for My children."

Then the soul spoke: "Tell me, Lord, about Your temptation so Your desire and mine may be united."

Our Lord said:

"Now hear how I am tempted.

My goodness and gentleness, faith and compassion so
overwhelm Me that I let them flow

Over the mountains of pride, the valleys of humility, the
thickets of discord,

And the smooth ways of purity.

My mercy is greater than the ill-will of wicked people,

And My righteousness is greater than all the devil's
wickedness."

Then the soul spoke:

"Lord, Your righteousness leads directly into the living
Truth and gives me unspeakable joy.

For wherever righteousness enters, truth rejoices."

11. (23.) The Power of Desire Makes One Speechless

Whoever has burned in Love's powerful Fire could
never want to cool herself with any kind of sin. "Beloved,"
said an exiled soul, "when shall You take delight in what
delights me?" Her Beloved answered: "I don't know what
you desire. What would you like?" She replied: "The

mighty power of desire has left me speechless." The Lord said: "Courting is not easy for young virgins, for they are naturally modest." Then the soul lamented: "Alas, Lord, You have been absent from me too long. If I could only win You so You could find no rest except with me, then love would begin. Then You would be forced to ask me to glow with love." Then He answered:

"Unblemished dove, let Me spare you, for the world cannot yet do without you."

The soul said:

"Lord, if it will only happen that in my heart's desire I might see You and throw my arms around You.

The Joy of Your Divine love will then pierce my soul as much as possible on this earth.

What I might suffer afterwards no human has ever seen.

I long for You so much that a thousand deaths matter little.

Now I will stand firm in faith to You.

If You can endure it, Lord, let me pursue You.

For I know that Love's first longing must come from You."

12. (24.) *Two Kinds of Persons Are Offered Two Kinds of Spirit By God*

There are two kinds of spiritual people on earth, and they are offered two kinds of spirit. God offers His Holy Spirit to those pure beings who live in faithful holiness. Thus two pure natures unite, God's glowing Fire and the growth of a loving soul. If there is a pure dwelling ready for humility, a bright light that can be seen from afar will be kindled. Then, O loving soul, you will be rich with treasures no one can take from you, even if you were the poorest of the poor. Through humility one becomes rich, through discipline and a well-ordered life one becomes noble and modest, through love one becomes worthy of praise, through un-deserved contempt one is elevated before God. Remember this, sister, and let no one drive you from your good habits, for by this you shall remain holy.

The devil also offers his spirit to those who in hatred and pride desire the worst.

They do not know that love leads to all good.

They become so poor from the devil's hatred and fury that it is impossible

They should ever again find or follow God's love.

True love praises God constantly.

Longing love gives the pure heart sweet sorrow.

Seeking love belongs to itself alone.

Understanding love loves all in common.

Enlightened love is mingled with sadness.

Selfless love bears fruit without effort.

It functions so quietly that the body knows nothing of it.

Clear love is quiet, in God alone

Seeing that both have one will and there is no creature that can separate them.

Knowledge writes this out of the everlasting book.

Gold is often spotted with copper just as falseness and vain honor blot out virtue from the human soul.

The vain soul to whom passing things are so dear that it never trembled before Love

Never heard God speak lovingly to it.

Alas, to such a soul this earthly life is all darkness.

1. (2.) This Book Has Come From God; The Soul Praises Him for Many Things; The Soul is Given Two Angels and Two Devils Along with Twelve Virtues to Strive Against the Flesh

All my life before I began this book and before a single word of it came from God into my soul, I was the simplest spiritual creature ever. I knew nothing of the devil's wickedness, the evil of the world, or the falseness of apparently spiritual people.

Now I must glorify God through speech and in the writing of this book. Unworthy sinner that I am, I was greeted by the Holy Spirit when I was twelve, so I could no longer give in to serious daily sin. The loving greeting came every day and caused me both love and sorrow; the sweetness and glory increased daily, continuing for thirty-one years.

I knew nothing of God except the usual Christian beliefs, and I tried to follow those diligently so my heart might become pure. God Himself will testify that I never consciously asked Him to give me the things I have written in this book. I had never dreamed that such things could happen to any human being.

Then through God's love I went to Magdeburg where I had only one friend. I was afraid that because of this friend my renunciation of the world and my love of God might be hindered.

But, God never left me. He brought me such sweetness of love, such heavenly knowledge, such inconceivable wonders, that I had little use for earthly things. Then I saw

the beautiful humanity of our Lord Jesus Christ with the
eyes of my soul, and I knew Him by His radiant face. I saw
the Holy Trinity, the Eternity of the Father, the work of the
Son, and the sweetness of the Holy Spirit. And I saw the
angel to whom I was dedicated at my baptism, and I saw
my devil.

Then our Lord said: "I will take this one angel from you
and give you two others instead. They shall care for you
when you are transported above the earth." When the soul
saw the two angels, it shrank into itself in humility and
flung itself at our Lord's feet and thanked Him fervently. It
complained that such spirits should be servants to someone
so unworthy. For one angel was a seraphim flaming with
love and blessed light toward the favored soul. The other
angel was a cherubim to guard the soul's gift of grace and to
order its wisdom.

Then our Lord allowed two devils to come from
Lucifer's school. As the soul looked at the most gruesome
devil, she shuddered; but then she too rejoiced in God and
gained courage. This devil was a deceiver disguised as an
angel. He nearly led me astray with his false cunning. He
came to me at Mass and said: "Look how beautiful I am.
Why don't you worship me?" The soul answered:
"Humanity shall worship God in wealth and in poverty."
Then he said: "Why don't you look up and see who I am?"
Then a beautiful but deceptive cloud that has led many
believers astray appeared in the air. The devil said: "If you
sit on that Throne, you shall be the Queen and I shall be
the most glorious youth beside you." But, the soul said: "I
would be a fool if I had found the best but took the worst."
Then he said: "Since you will not give yourself to me, I will
worship you because you are so holy and I am so humble."
The soul replied: "No grace will be given to you for wor-
shipping a speck of dirt." Then he showed me marks like
five wounds on his hands, feet, and side, and said: "Now do

you see who I am? If you will live by my advice, I will give
you great honor. If you tell others about this grace, much
good will come out of it." The soul was displeased at this
fable, but she heard it willingly because it showed her his
real identity. "You tell me you are the Son of the living
God," she said. "Tell me, then, who is He who now here as
the Son of the Living God lies in the hands of the true
priest?" When he started to go, she said:

I command you in the name of Almighty God to hear me.
I know your intention:
If I were to tell humanity what is in my heart, all would
    go well for a while.
Then you would insist that the game must stop.
You would do this so I might fall into doubt and despair,
    unbelief, impurity, and eternal sorrow.
You would also make me pretend to be holy, you wicked
    deceiver.
While God stands by me, all your tricks and cunning are
    in vain.
Then he cried: "Let me away from you. I will never
    bother you again."

The other devil given me was a peace-breaker, a master
of secret impurity. But, God had forbidden this one to come
near me himself. Instead he sent messengers to me who
distorted good things and took from my honor as much as
they could by slandering me. The devil came also where
devout people were gathered together and spoke to them
in wicked ways about evil things. Because this had never
happened to me before, I could not help being troubled.

One night when I was praying before my sleep, this
devil came flying through the air, looking down on the sinful earth, and laughing in an evil rage. The soul asked why
he laughed and what he was trying to do. He said: "I rejoice
that, even though I cannot torment you myself, I can find
many who will take on the appearance of angels and

torment you for me. I am the guardian of spiritual people, and I seek two kinds of weakness in them that will separate them quickly from God. The first is secret impurity. The second is hidden hatred in open discord. That sin is useful to me for it is the foundation of long-practiced evil and leads to the loss of holiness." Then the soul said: "You have in your nature nothing good about you; why do you boast about your wickedness?" He said: "God has so bound me that I can do nothing unless He allows me to do so."

Unblessed creature that I am, I had committed such great sins in my childhood, that if I had not repented, I would have had to spend ten years in Purgatory. But now, dear Lord, if I should die, I would gladly endure there for Your love.

I do not say that myself, Love commands me to say it.
When I came to the spiritual life and withdrew from the
    world,
I looked at my body.
It was heavily armed against my poor soul with plenty of
    strength and with the full powers of nature.
I saw it was my enemy and saw also
That if I wanted to escape everlasting death, I must con-
    quer self completely,
And that would be a difficult struggle.
Then I looked to the weapons of my soul
And saw that they were the glorious suffering and death
    of our Lord Jesus Christ.
That was my protection.
My youth aimed heavy blows at my body: sighing, weep-
    ing, confession, fasting, watching,
Recollection, discipline, and prayer.
I must practice these constantly.
With these weapons of my soul I so painfully conquered the body that for twenty years I was always tired, ill and weak; first, from remorse and sorrow, then, from good

desires and spiritual effort. I had many days of bodily sickness. But, God's mighty love struck me so powerfully with its wonders that I could no longer keep silent. I exclaimed: "Merciful God, what have You seen in me? You know I am a fool, a sinner, and a poor creature in body and soul. You should have given these things to the wise, then You would have been praised." But our Lord was angry with me. "Tell me," he said, "are you truly Mine?" "Yes, Lord, I do ask You that I can be truly Yours." "Can I not do with you what I will, then?" "Yes, beloved Lord, even if I should become nothing." Then our Lord said: "You shall follow Me and trust Me in all things. You shall have a long illness, and I will take care of you Myself. All that you need in body and soul I will give to you."

Then I went in humble shame to my confessor, told him all this, and asked for his guidance. He said I should go forward with great joy; God, who had called me, would watch over me. Then he commanded me to do that about which I often weep for shame when I look at my unworthiness: write this book out of God's heart and mouth. This book has thus come lovingly from God and not from the human senses.

2. (3.) *How Sinners Fall Away from God; Of Three Gifts of Wisdom; Of a Stone; Of Praise of a Maiden Who Represents Holy Church*

As one soothes a child, so one subdues suffering, so also does our Lord when He says: "Those who have nothing good in them can never enter My Kingdom. Those who are never satisfied with passing things must be satisfied with everlasting hunger. Woe to those who have something to which their heart clings and who set themselves up above

their fellows. They shall fall away from Me into the bottomless pit."

Holy Knowledge answers that God has given us three
gifts of true wisdom whereby we can satisfy ourselves and
guard against all harm.

The first gift is priestly wisdom and Christian learning. I
saw a Stone with the eyes of my eternity and without effort.
It was like a great multicolored mountain, and it tasted
sweetly of heavenly herbs. I asked the sweet stone who it
was, and it said, "I am Jesus." Then I went lovingly out of
myself and laid my head on Him. I saw that He shut out all
darkness and thàt He was filled inwardly with everlasting
light.

A lovely young virgin, the companion of our Lady, stood
on this Stone. Her feet are adorned with jasper. It drives all
greed from desire, imparts pure taste, excites heavenly
hunger, and wipes away all darkness from the eyes. It is
called Christian Faith.

The virgin stood on two feet. One is her bond with God;
the other is absolution through Divine power. All Christian
priests have these two. The maiden holds in her right hand
a chalice with red wine which she alone drinks with
unspeakable joy. This is the blood of the everlasting Son; it
fills her spirit so that she gives us much sound teaching. In
her left hand she holds a fiery sword; golden cymbals hang
from it which sound so sweetly that all who joyfully honor
the Holy Trinity must come to them.

I asked the virgin why she held the sword in her left
hand and the chalice in her right. She said: "I must threat-
en all human beings until their last day; then God must
strike His blow. And I must offer Christ's blood with my
right hand, for Christ is called to honor His Father." The
virgin has great power in her hands by which she draws to
herself everything God has chosen and throws away all the
devil has given. Her face is so radiant and beautiful that she

appears more beautiful every time I look at her. Her eyes overflow with happiness just as the rising sun sends the rosy dawn before it. Then comes a description of a crown and a tower:

The blessed who live in it don't need to engage fully in battle.

The only ones who can come up into the tower are those from whom love has taken their earthly will.

The crown has many precious stones on its pinnacles.

These are the ones who have already gone from earth to the heavenly Kingdom.

I saw a spring of living water springing up in this virgin's heart.

Heathen children, leprous and blind, were carried to this spring.

Above the spring stood a very holy man, and he was the only one who could draw water from it.

This was John the Baptist.

He washed the children in the spring, and they were cleansed and received their sight.

Then I asked the virgin who she was:

"I am the one you love, and I am your companion.

I am Holy Church.

We each have a bridegroom; he is the priest who looks so lovingly upon the blessed maids."

The second wisdom is of the natural senses, with it we can both lose and gain.

Many foolish lay people, false priests, and perverted spiritual people live in this wisdom.

None are so holy as to be able to guard themselves against these three.

Their nature is so full of mischief that it perverts everything good.

No one becomes spiritual through these gifts unless she is willing to be a fool for God's love.

Pure holy simplicity is the mother of true knowledge of
   God.
What does it mean that a person has much money?
Money buys nothing but hunger and thirst,
Contempt and everlasting sorrow of heart.
The third wisdom is Grace:
It suffices for all God's gifts.
It is never so rich in its own sight that it does not compare
   itself to the smallest creatures.
It does not complain because of its adversity but delights
   in God's will alone.
It does not permit even one virtue to be shut out by its
   door.

3. (4.) Of Two Different Ways, One Goes Down to Hell and the Other Up to Heaven

The riches of passing things are like an unfaithful guest.
Holy Poverty bears a precious burden before God.
Self-conceit does not stop to think of the harm it does.
Constancy contains all virtues.
Stupidity is sufficient to itself alone,
Wisdom can never learn enough.
Anger brings great darkness to the soul,
Holy Gentleness is sure of all grace.
Pride always wants to be first,
Humility never rests until it can serve all creatures.
Empty honor is deaf and blind before God,
Undeserved contempt sanctifies all God's children.

4. (5.) Of Sin and Our Future Falls; Of Earthly Things; Of Heaven; How God's Gift Shall Stand Openly Before Our Eyes

Lord, my sin through which I have lost You stands before
    my eyes like the highest mountain
And has for a long time put darkness and distance
    between You and me.
Love above all love draw me again to You.
But, future falls are ever before my eyes like the mouth
    of a fiery dragon eager to swallow me up.
My only Good, please help me now so I may flow sinless
    unto You.
Lord, my earthly being stands before me like a dusty
    acre on which little good has grown.
Sweet Jesus Christ, send me now the fruitful rain of Your
    Humanity and the gentle dew of the Holy Spirit
So I may plead my heart's sorrow.
Your everlasting Kingdom lies open before my eyes like
    a wedding feast, a noble wedding, and an
Everlasting banquet.
True lover, draw Your lovesick bride ceaselessly to Your
    side.
All the gifts I have ever received from You stand before
    me as a heavy reproach,
For Your highest gift humbles me.
Then God who gives everything answers:
"Love shall melt away your mountain;
Your enemies shall win no victory over you.
A hot sun has scorched your acre, but its fruit has not
    been destroyed.
You shall live as a new bride in My Kingdom.
I will greet you with the kiss of love, and all My Godhead
    shall sweep through your soul.

My three-fold vision shall play ceaselessly in your two-
fold heart.
Where then is your mourning?
If you should pray for a thousand years, I would never
give you cause for a single sigh."

5. (6.) No One Can Ever Disturb God's Elect; Real Remorse is Pardoned By God's Grace

A troubled soul asked me to pray for him. In His mercy,
God heard me and said: "There is no lamb so white or so
pure that its wool never becomes stained. No one may dis-
turb My elect. Of this, I have assured this troubled soul in
three things. First, I am compassionate regarding his sin.
Second, I have given him My Grace. Third, I will never
allow unfaithful people to have any power over him."

Then I prayed: "Lord, he still fears that You have not
entirely forgiven his sin." God answered: "That is impossible. Whoever is sorry for his sin and laments his sin, I give
him My Grace and forgive his sin. Whoever grieves so
much for sin so that he would rather die than sin again, after
this life he shall be condemned to no further punishment
even if he sins every day."

6. (7.) How a Free Spirit Speaks to God in Utter Love

Lord, because I have been subject to all creatures, You
have drawn me up from this earth to You. Because I have
no earthly treasure, thus I have no earthly heart. For You,
Lord, are my treasure, You are my heart, You alone are all
my good, and I am indifferent to everything else.

7. (12.) How the Bride United with God Refuses All Creaturely Comfort and Accepts It; How She Sinks Under Suffering

The Bride of God who has dwelt in the Holy Trinity's sanctuary said: "Get away from me, all earthly creatures, for you bring me pain and cannot comfort me." The creatures asked why. The Bride said: "My Love has left me while I rested beside Him and slept." But the creatures said: "Can't this world and all your blessings comfort you?" "No," said the Bride, "I see the serpent of falsehood and false wisdom creeping in to all the joy of this world. I also see the hook of greed in the bait of vain sweetness by which it snares many."

"Can't even the Kingdom of Heaven comfort you?" asked the creatures. "No, the Kingdom in itself is not alive if the living God is not there."

"O Bride, can the saints comfort you?" "No," she said, "for if they were separated from the living Godhead that flows through them, they would weep more bitterly than I, for they have risen higher than I and live more deeply in God."

"Can the Son of God comfort you?"

Yes, I ask Him when we shall go into the flowery meadows of heavenly knowledge.

And I pray to Him fervently that He unlock for me the swirling flood that plays about the Holy Trinity,

For the soul lives on that alone.

If I am to be comforted according to the merit to which God has raised me,

Then His breath must draw me effortlessly into Himself.

For the sun that plays upon the living Godhead radiates the clear water of a joyful humanity.

And the sweet desire of the Holy Spirit comes to us both.

Nothing can satisfy me except God alone, for without Him I am as dead.

Yet I would gladly sacrifice the joy of His presence, if He could be greatly honored by my doing so.

For if I, unworthy as I am, cannot praise God with all my might,

Then I shall send all creatures to Heaven's Court, and command them to praise God for me.

With all their wisdom, their love, their beauty, all their desires, as they were created, sinless by God,

To sing with all the sweetness of their voices as they now sing.

If only I could witness this praise, I would no longer be sorrowful.

Neither can I bear a single consolation except what Love alone can give me. I love my earthly friends in a heavenly fellowship, and I love my enemies with a heavenly longing for their salvation. God has enough of all good things except dialogue with the soul, for of that He can never have enough.

When this wonder and consolation had continued for eight years, God wished to comfort me more powerfully, far above what I deserved. "No, dear Lord, do not raise me up too high," cried this unworthy soul. "Even this low place is too much for me. Gladly I will stay here to honor you." Then the soul fell down below the ill-fated souls who had forfeited their rewards, and it seemed good to her to do so. Our Lord followed her there. God's appearance was beautiful and glorious to all in that place.

After this God's Forsakenness so surrounded the soul that it cried: "Welcome, blessed Forsakenness. I am glad I was born and that you, Constancy, are my chambermaid, for you bring me unaccustomed joy and inconceivable wonders and sweetness beyond what I can bear. But Lord, You must take this sweetness from me and forsake me. It is well for me, O faithful Lord, that after love's transformation I can bear forsakenness in my soul."

Blessed Forsakenness of God, how lovingly I am bound to you. You strengthen my will in suffering and make dear to me this poor body's long difficult waiting. The nearer I come to you, the greater and more wonderful God appears to me. Lord, even in the depths of my humility, I cannot sink away from You completely:

I lost You so easily in my pride,
But the more deeply I sink,
The more sweetly I drink of You.

8. (13.) I See, Hear, and Feel in All My Members the Writing of This Book

I cannot write nor do I wish to write. But I see this book with the eyes of my soul, hear it with the ears of my eternal spirit, and feel in every part of my body the power of the Holy Spirit.

9. (15.) Pure Love Has Four Essentials; If You Give Yourself to God, He Will Give Himself to You

Pure love of God has four essentials that never change. The first is growing desire, the second is unceasing anxiety, the third is burning love in body and soul, the fourth is constant union combined with strict watchfulness. No one can reach this state unless she makes a complete exchange with God. If God give you everything that is yours, within and without, He will truly give you all that is His.

When the blessed hour has passed in which God has granted the loving soul His precious consolation,

Then the soul is so full of delight that everything which might hurt a loveless soul seems good to it.

Are you displeased? Then you might fear that the devil has anointed you.

10. (16.) Great Love Has More Than Ten Parts; A Two-fold Lament

This is the nature of great love—it does not flow with tears, but it burns in the great Fire of Heaven. In this fire it flows swiftly and yet remains in itself in great stillness. It rises almost up to God, yet remains small in itself. It grasps much and retains little. Most blessed Love, where are the ones who know you? They are entirely illuminated in the Holy Trinity; they can no longer live in themselves. Such blessed souls can never fall into mortal sin. Why? Because God so completely surrounds and penetrates them that the more they are tempted, the stronger they become. Why? Because the longer they struggle and continue to love, the greater God appears to them, and the smaller and more sinful they seem to themselves. Why? Because the holier the love, the greater the anxiety, the more numerous the consolation, the more constant the fear. But the loving soul does not fear with dread; it fears nobly. Of two things I can never lament sufficiently: the first is that God is so forgotten in the world; the second is that spiritual people are so imperfect. Thus, there will be many falls, for the perfect never fall.

11. (19.) The Manifold Mission of Love

O blessed Love, whose mission was and is to unite God
  and the human soul,

That shall be your mission without end, as it was without
  beginning.

I greet you, Love, only beware lest I complain about you
  to my glorious Lord.

For if He is absent from me too long, then I will grow too
  cold.

Save me from that, O Queen of Love, you who have led
  me to God

So that I am joyfully bound to Him.

Love, help me to expire in His arms in which I am now
  embraced.

For His sake I would happily endure the pains of death
  in my sinful body.

Love, you have the greatest power above all virtues forever.

For I thank God that you heal my heart's sorrows.

I no longer have any virtues; they serve me, yet they are
  truly His.

That I should do anything good without God is much
  harder for me than death.

I dare not take all that I have to say about Love to
  myself,

It is God who directs these words to all His elect treasured in His heart.

Those whom this concerns know well that Love makes
  empty hearts overflow—

Even more when we must struggle without assurance,
  unready for Love's play.

Now Love, goodnight, for I am going to sleep.

Alleluia!

12. (24.) *How God Receives Souls in Heaven*

The Kingdom of Heaven has many beautiful gates and yet has none. For the gates are the glorious rewards with which God receives each soul and opens the whole of Heaven to God's blissful bride. He Himself goes down through all the choirs to meet the soul, and the heavenly hosts follow Him in order according to the greatness of the reward each soul can receive. Thus the soul comes joyfully out of Purgatory and many glorious angels follow her. At the gate of Heaven the lovers, God and the soul, meet. The noble glance with which God receives her has such power that she can think no longer of past sorrows or pain.

It is God's will that a simple crown of the Kingdom is placed on her head in the gate. There He leads her in honor; therefore it is called the Crown of the Kingdom. Sinners who have forfeited grace but to whom God sends remorse have no other honor as reward.

God crowns three kinds of virgins, widows, and married people with His fatherly hand. After He has received them with all honor, He crowns them. The widows and the married couples He crowns sitting in His great glory. For the virgins He stands up and crowns them as a Mighty Monarch. He greets them inwardly with His living Godhead; He honors them outwardly with His Almighty humanity. He adorns them with the generosity of the Holy Spirit. He rewards them ceaselessly with His complete Holy Trinity according to their rank and standing in His Kingdom, for all that they bring with them. He thanks them specially that they have willed to come, while they praise Him joyfully that He has delivered them from everlasting death.

13. (28.) Of the Fivefold Power of Love

This book was begun in love and shall also end in love. For there is nothing so wise, nor so holy, nor so beautiful, nor so strong, nor so perfect as love. Thus spoke our Lord: "Speak, Father. I will now be silent as You were silent in the mouth of Your Son when He burned because of love for an ailing humanity. My humanity trembled at the world's falseness, for it rewarded Me with a bitter death."

BOOK
V

1. Of the Three Kinds of Repentance

There are three kinds of repentance the sinner makes in turning to the Cross, which took our sins away.

The first repentance is for sin. This is threefold: bitterness of the heart from which the sins have come; shame in the senses, which realized the sin; and a true picture of the life the creature has ruined. The heavenly Father reconciles this repentance and the sinning soul, and delivers the soul from the pains of everlasting Hell.

The second repentance is that of confession. It has three characteristics: diligent effort, steady assurance, and victory over all temptation.

The third repentance is that of love. This alone is true to God, for to dishonor God hurts the soul more than its own hurt or sorrow. It would rather go down to Hell with love in its heart than grieve its Beloved by mortal sin. Such loving repentance sanctifies the soul on earth and raises it up in honor before God. When the soul is in this state, God is dearer to it than it is to itself, and it is heartily sorry for sin.

To the blessed who have these three kinds of repentance, God sends His radiant Spirit to shine ceaselessly in their souls. The glance that passes between God and the loving soul shines so brightly from both and has great power before all who are in Heaven, Purgatory, or Hell that even the angels seek intimacy with the soul and wander gently down to it in the same gleaming splendor and unspeakable love.

Such is the noble way of the repentant soul in this poor body, for the angels and the love of the soul are one nature of inborn purity in God.

Therefore the noble radiance streams down to reflect
love anew.

The angels given us in baptism may not tend this burning
love,

For God has not given them the necessary fervor.

They are given to us to tend our virtues.

Their presence and our courage sanctify everything we
do and drive away the cunning of the devil and his power
over our senses. The fiery splendor that shines from the
Holy Trinity into the loving soul so frightens the devils that
they never attempt to pass through the holy beams. When
they become aware of a loving soul in human form, they
disappear beneath the earth and they do not pollute the air
where the blessed dwell without mortal sin. Thus we must
ascend to God in the true Christian faith; then the devils
lose all their power and flee from us.

2. Of Two Kinds of Suffering and Their Uses

I thank God for all my blessings and I am sorrowful for
my past life, for God does not send suffering for no pur-
pose. As long as the creature sins, she requires suffering as
much as virtue. The suffering that the soul inflicts on itself
according to God's will and according to priestly counsel is
of great use.

But, the suffering God Himself sends us through His
friends or enemies is as much more noble and useful as
God Himself is nobler than any suffering.

Christ does not redeem us through the agony He volun-
tarily endured, but by teaching us how to serve Him with
works and suffering. He redeemed us through the suffering
inflicted on His innocence by His enemies and by His
death at which no one was His true friend except Mary, his
mother; she was truly and inwardly one with Him and she
stood by Him outwardly.

Because faithless people overloaded me with suffering, God gave me this comfort: "Behold, no one can escape suffering, for it purifies humankind from hour to hour for its many sins." Then I saw a dreadful group of sins as if all mountains, stones, raindrops, grass, trees, leaves, and sand were living beings who tried to prevent us from reaching God. I cannot describe the living dust of sin; the suffering we bear secretly in our bodies gives witness to that.

The second kind of suffering, bitterness, protects us from future falls, for that pure heart that often trembles before it carries the spirit of God secretly within itself.

The third, the nobility of suffering, makes us worthy to receive God's grace. Even though I accept my need and trouble and my earthly comfort with fear and a trembling heart, God is always there with His consolation.

3. God Will One Day Weigh All Innocent Suffering

On the Last Day Jesus Christ will set before His Father a glorious pair of scales. His holy deeds and innocent suffering will be weighed against all the innocent suffering, contempt and sorrow that anyone has ever suffered for Him. Thus a just balance is secured: Those who have the most in the scales to be weighed against Christ's suffering will have the most joy.

4. Wondrous Love Has Many Powers; Of Fourfold Humility; Of Seven Ornaments of the Loving Soul

O wondrous love of God, You Great and Holy Might, You enliven the soul and teach the senses, and give full power to all virtue.

It is good for me, poor fool that I am, that I joyfully kept You before my eyes.

Love, You are full of delight and to be praised in all Your works.

I know in my soul all virtues are subject to You.

But deepening humility, unstained by pride of spirit, and inborn or acquired purity are two virtues that must go with love, even though they are subject to it.

Love wanders through the senses and storms with all virtues on the soul. While love grows in the soul, it rises eagerly up to God and overflows towards Glory. Love melts through the soul into the senses, so the body may have its share of it, for love is drawn into all things.

Can anyone living in God have evil habits? No, for the untainted Love of God has great power. But the soul is never so mightily saturated by Divine Love that it is not often tempted by earthly things.

A soul saturated by false things can never receive true love. When love is fullgrown in the soul it must rise as far as possible to human nature, for love is measured. If it were not measured, many pure hearts would break for joy.

When the soul walks with love and with eager desire for God in its heart, and when it has come to the Mount of powerful love and blissful knowledge, it descends carefully so it will not fall over a precipice. Illumined by the fire of its long love, overpowered by the Holy Trinity's embrace, it begins to sink and to cool as the sun from its highest zenith sinks down into the night. Thus God knows this is the way it is with the soul and the body. The richly loving soul sinks down into a profound humility. Because of the noble nature that fills God and the soul with one mind, the soul welcomes whatever God does to it in love. The soul refrains from looking at all things with delight so it may better win God's praise. It sinks swiftly to the lowest place God has in His power. How can I even dare to name this place which humility cannot even recognize?

The first humility lies externally in housing and clothing. Clothes and dwellings should be clean and properly cared for, so that they reflect the manner of spiritual people.

The second humility is seen in our attitudes toward others. We should be loving to others in all things. From this God's holy love will grow.

The third humility applies to the senses. In this, all things should be used properly and loved appropriately.

The fourth humility lies in the soul. It chases the soul up into the heavens and draws it down again into the depths. It leads the soul to all creatures and says: "Look, these creatures are all better than you are." It leads the soul to a place under Lucifer's tail where it can sink no lower. Even if it wanted to stay in this place and honor God in its humble desire, it could not do so.

So closely is the loving soul bound to humble love that it is no longer afraid or ashamed except in moderation, as one might stand in fear and awe of Heaven.

Yet the poor body must be afraid and ashamed of the darkness of its heart and the sickness of its outward senses, since it is not yet transformed by death. But the soul is just as safe in its body as in the Kingdom of Heaven, though not so certain; just as daring, but not so strong; just as powerful, but not so constant; just as loving, but not so joyful; just as gentle, but not so rich; just as holy, but not yet so sinless; just as content, but not yet so complete. This all applies to the soul saturated by humility because of its love for God.

When the soul has thus climbed to the highest it can reach while still in the body, and has sunk to the lowest depths it can find, then it is fullgrown in virtue and holiness. But it still must wait patiently to be adorned with suffering. Thus the soul takes its stand on faithfulness and looks with wisdom on all things. It lacks nothing so long as it can win God's praises.

5. (6.) How the Soul Praises the Holy Trinity; A Prayer

Lord Jesus Christ, You came forth without beginning from the Eternal Father's heart. You Who were born of the flesh of a pure Virgin and Who are one Spirit, one Will, one Wisdom, one Might, one Power with the Father are over all that ever was eternally.

O, Lord, as I, of all people most unworthy, also came forth spiritually from Your heart and side, and as I, O Lord, God and man, am united with the Spirit of both, thus I, a poor sad being, say:

Lord and heavenly Father, You are my heart.
Lord Jesus Christ, You are my body.
Lord Holy Spirit, you are my breath.
Lord Holy Trinity, You are my only refuge and my
   everlasting Peace.

6. (7.) How God Praises the Soul in Return

You are a foundation of My Divine Being.
You are an honor of virginal constancy.
You are a flower of great delight.
You are a vanquisher of evil spirits.
You are a mirror of eternal contemplation.

7. (17.) A Sinner's Praise, Prayer, and Greeting

Living God, I greet You, for You are mine above all
other things.
I am endlessly happy that I can speak freely with You.
When my enemies pursue me, I flee to Your arms.
There I can speak my sorrow as You listen to me.
You know well that You can bring music from all the
strings of my soul.
I hope this might now begin to happen so that You
might have bliss!
I am an unworthy bride, but You are my noble Love.
Therefore I rejoice eternally.
Remember how You are able to court the pure soul in
Your embrace and bring it soon to pass in me,
Unworthy as I am of You.
Lord, lift me up to You, so I shall be pure and clear.
If You leave me to myself, I must ever remain in dark-
ness and heaviness.

8. (18.) How God Answers

My answering greeting is a heavenly flood so powerful
that I give Myself to you in all My Power,
And your human life is ended.
Therefore, you see that I must restrain My Might and
hide the full glory of My Splendor
And hold you longer in your earthly misery, until sud-
denly all your sweetness
Rises up to the heights of everlasting merit.
And My music shall sound sweetly in your ears, after you
have paid the cost with your faithful love.

Yet I will begin early to tune My heavenly strings in your
   soul
So you may wait more patiently:
For noble brides and knightly lords can only be trained
   at great cost,
After long and careful preparation.

9. (19.) How Sin Drives Humanity in Seventeen Ways

Sin drives a people so far from God that they could never
return to Him if it were not for the great power exerted by
the Holy Trinity. Vanity is the first sin that begins to drive
people from God. If we do not conquer it, impurity raises
its head. If we do not conquer impurity, then follow greed,
indolence, lying, perjury, anger, slander, pride, hatred,
revenge, despondency, shamelessness, and unbelief.

Such people receive all God gives them with such anger
that one not dare speak to them, and their own behavior
and speech is so wrong and mixed with untruths that the
Holy Spirit cannot be found in their words. If their behavior is sometimes praiseworthy, that is only a false sign.

Rejoice, perfect soul, for you alone are like God, and that
   is just.
For you drink much bitterness with divine patience and
   without sin.
You will often be distressed because of your enemies.
Though bright perfection shines in heavenly flowers,
   and they bloom happily in solitude
And reach up to the heights in noble beauty,
The root of their constancy is in the Holy Spirit, ever
   fresh and green.

10. (20.) A Praise of God in Eight Things; Of the Offering of Sin

God, You are glorious and mysterious as the morning dew.
Fruit of Mary's flower and flower of embracing love that
    bore this earthly love,
Redeemer and Comforter!
Those humbled in the heart whose overweening pride
    insults You,
Take daily all I have.
When You have poured in Your love upon my sin, take
    the sacred overflow,
So back to You I go.

11. (21.) Why Humanity is Rejected and Yet Loved

Thus speak the senses of the ones who have experi-
enced the Truth: Lord, my body is mortified by the
changes brought about by sin. Therefore, Your enemies
have put me put of their sight like a corrupt body. But, my
soul is alive in You, and I am thus loved by Your friends.
Beloved Bridegroom, sweet Jesus Christ, I bless You without ceasing in my heart for all earthly things. I pray that You
will protect me from being tainted by them. For they are
not holy, but they interfere with my highest allegiance to
You. I could not bear that, so I must wage war on them.

12. (22.) Of Seven Demands of the Law

The noblest joy of the senses, the holiest peace of the
heart, and the most loving radiance of all good works comes
from the fact that the creature puts its heart into what it does.

Here our Lord speaks and teaches me about seven things the blessed must have.

The first demand is righteousness in the present. If I see my friend act wrongly toward my and God's enemy, then I blame my friend and lovingly help my enemy.

The second is compassion in need. If I see my friend and my enemy in equal need, I shall help them both equally.

The third is faithfulness in friendship. I will never reprove my friend except for her unfaithful soul.

The fourth is help in secret need. We should seek and find the stranger, the sick and the prisoner, and comfort them with friendly words and prayers and beg them to tell You their secret needs so You can help them.

No one should ever leave the sick or outcast without tears and sighs and compassion:

This does not fit spiritual people and sets them away from God.

They lose His sweet intimacy and do not realize they incur His judgment.

The fifth demand is that one should be silent in anger. Do not speak words that arise from a proud and angry heart. Not doing so finds endless grace in God.

The sixth is that one shall be filled with truth. The person who is full of truth is the one whose heart in its best moments does not give way to any faults. This person rejoices that God's eye sees right into her heart and has nothing of which to be ashamed, even if all humanity were to look into her heart.

The seventh is that one shall be a sworn enemy of lying. We should rebuke lying in everyone and not hide it in ourselves.

We shall practice and achieve these seven virtues against the will of our rebellious flesh

And against the pull and weakness of the senses,

Otherwise we shall not reach them.

The soul's nobility toward all good gives us the gentleness of God's love.

In its vain way, our sinful nature neglects many a divine day.

When we think of the blessed hours

That God, out of the depths of His heart, His wisdom, and His joyful nature

Ceaselessly pours forth all good,

And out of His sweet mouth spiritually tempers our souls,

Then we must be ashamed of our evil habits and our faithless hearts.

We must also be ashamed of our senses, for we make such poor use

Of God's numerous noble gifts.

And they bring back so little fruit to the place where God's very heart flowed out over us.

Goodwill brings all virtue to its rightful end,

A task for which the body alone is not strong enough.

13. (30.) Of Twenty Powers of God's Love

Dear Love of God, embrace my soul.

It would grieve me above all sorrow to be parted from You.

Therefore, I pray You will not let my love grow cold,

For if I were not conscious of You, everything I do would be useless.

Love, you make pain and need seem sweet to me, and You give God's children comfort and wisdom.

Bond of Love, Your hand is powerful.

It binds both young and old, makes heavy burdens seem light, and little sins seem large.

You willingly serve all creatures for love alone.

Sweet love of God, if I should sleep too long and neglect
all good things,

Awaken me and sing, for the sweet music with which
You touch my soul delights me.

Love, fling me down under You, for I would gladly be
vanquished.

I would find comfort if You should take my life from me.

Most gentle Love of God, You spare me too much and I
lament that.

Love, Your wondrous greeting fills my heart.

The pain You cause me helps me live without sin,

And Your steady devotion brings me much sweet sorrow.

Divine Love, how can I be patient if I lack You?

Yet, Your absence gives me a high and heavenly courage.

Wondrous Love, she whom You teach is happy

For it is a joyful humility that begs You to turn from the
soul.

Love, how ever small You find the one who seeks and
diligently pursues You in all things.

Inviting You with love's eagerness to flee from her.

Yet, there are many who call You who turn away from You
in their works.

Your coming and going, O Love, are equally welcome to
the well-ordered soul.

You have achieved with heartfelt love that task that God
began in us.

Your noble clearness that stands as a mirror between God
and the pure soul,

Awakens burning love in the virgin for Jesus, her dear
Love.

Your holy compassion causes the devils much distress.

Your sweet peace brings gentle feelings and pure habits.

Your holy sufficiency leads free spirits willingly to poverty.

Love, Your true perfection does not complain of misfor-
tune or heavy labors.

14. (31.) Of the Powers of Love; How No Creature May Fully Express the Soul's Longing for God

Love, Your light is broad in the soul. Your gleam is radiant, Your glory inconceivable, Your wisdom infinite, Your bounty swift, Your grasp powerful, Your being perfect, Your flow gentle, Your riches great, Your work faithful and Your discernment holy.

Because You penetrate the soul with all these, You raise it up to fly with the wings of a dove, to long with the eagerness of an eagle, and to follow Your fiery radiance up to Heaven.

Thus speaks Truth: "Lord, the longing I have to follow You, the wisdom I receive in the flight of love, the union I grasp in Your will, the constancy I receive from Your gifts, the sweet memories when I think of You, and the repentant love I have from You are so rich and before Your eyes so powerful, that if You did not know it, no creature could tell You half the intensity of my longing, the extent of my suffering, the hunting of my heart, and the uplifting of my soul to be at one with You eternally."

15. (35.) How Mechthild Thanks and Praises God and Prays for Three Kinds of People and Herself

Merciful Father, God in Heaven, draw my soul flowingly and untroubled to You,

And flow toward me, O Lord, with all the joy that is Yours.

Thus the soul loves to offer You praise for all Your goodness.

Draw me by the power of Your Holy Trinity into the
sweet stream of love,

So that in praising You I may turn to good account all
Your merciful gifts.

I ask nothing of You, Lord, that would not lead me to
Your praise.

For all Your faithfulness, Father of all good, I, a poor sinner, thank You with my suffering body, my outcast soul, my
sinful heart, my sorrowful senses, and with my whole being,
so despised in this world. These alone are mine, O Father,
with Your dear Son Jesus Christ and in fellowship with all
creatures. All these were untainted before the Fall, and
when they return they shall be reinstated to the highest.

I praise You with these this day, for You have shown true
protection to my poor body and outcast soul. I thank You
for all the merciful gifts You have been pleased to give me.
With all creatures I would praise You in and for all things
that have flowed unspotted from Your generous heart. With
all these I pray that You will glorify Yourself by a conversion
of those sinners who today lie in mortal sin. I pray to You
for all the suffering souls who through our sins have gone to
Purgatory. May we carefully guard ourselves from such sins.
I pray to You for the salvation, protection, and perfecting of
Your Holy Spirit, in all those by name who have helped me
to bear the misery of my body and soul. I pray to You
through Your Son Jesus that You will change the suffering
of my spiritual poverty and turn the bitter drink to honey in
the palate of my soul. I pray to You, for the eternal honor of
the Christian Faith, that You protect us from all false ways
with Your Divine Wisdom. Strengthen our spirits, O Lord,
so we may rest in Your Holy Trinity.

I pray that all those who persecute Christians may yet
come to know You openly before all people. I pray for truth
in the false people in ruling positions and that they will
have compassion for the innocent. I pray that You, Eternal

Consoler, would comfort all sorrowing souls who must this day part with fear from their bodies, and that You, their Preserver, would keep them safe and give them everlasting life. I pray for spiritual clarity, constancy, and strength in upholding Divine truth in all things, and for those who possess spiritual power through Your love. I pray You will give me true thankfulness at all times, for all Your gifts that help those who through love for You carry heavy burdens.

I ask You, holy God, for a compassionate view of my useless life, for union with You in my soul, for the sacrament of Your Holy Body to help me on my way, that at the end it may be the last food of soul and body. I also pray that You would bend Yourself toward me in the painful parting of my soul from my sinful body; that all my enemies may part sadly from me, and that I, according to Your sweet will and desire, may see You without ceasing; that my soul's eyes may rest on Your Godhead, and that Your sweet love may sweep through my soul.

Through our Lord Jesus Christ your Son. Amen.

BOOK
VI

1. (4.) Of Discretion and Fear Whereby the Senses are Protected from Earthly Things

Alas for me, poor wretch, I am sorrowful before God that I am now worse than I was thirty years ago. For those who helped me then bear my homeless life did not after all help me so much, if it was only my body that was to recover. I must always set two guards between my soul and earthly things that they may not tempt my body more than I can bear. One guard is Prudence, who orders all needful things according to God's will, so that the human heart sits lightly to all earthly things.

My other guard is Holy Fear, which, through God's wisdom, ensures that my soul does not smile on the earthly gifts I am given. It receives them as a temptation, fearing greed or vain honor. These darken the souls of many praiseworthy spiritual persons. They so completely lose the light of discretion, the fire of love, and the touch of God's sweetness, peace, and compassion that they hardly recognize these gifts.

Our Lord spoke: "They speak in fine parables; they say they only want to love earthly things and draw many possessions to themselves in order to love Me better. But they serve themselves more than they serve Me. Those who seek their own comfort and happiness belong to themselves alone." But everyone ought to be a Christ to herself so that God, not herself, lives in her. To the holy person who lives completely in God, it matters not what God sends—poverty or riches. For God with His power sometimes casts a person into holy poverty in the same way as He cast His beloved Son down from Heaven onto the highway and into the Crib. In the same way the Lord drives His chosen friends from all earthly comfort so they may hunger for heavenly comfort. A truly holy person fears earthly comfort more than earthly need, because her home is in Heaven and her prison is in this world. Thus our Lord said: "Whoever knows and loves the nobility of My freedom cannot bear to love Me alone in Myself; He must love Me also in the creatures, though I remain always close to his soul."

2 (5.) Of Love and Longing; The Beauty of Creatures Gives Knowledge with Sorrow

The first knowledge God granted me after His touch of love and flow of desire came to me with sadness. Whenever I saw anything beautiful or dear to me, I began to sigh, to weep, to think, to lament, and to speak thus to all things: "Beware, this is not your Love who has greeted your heart, enlightened your senses, and so wonderfully captured your soul. But this infinite delight in earthly things cannot drive you from your Love. I will love God, not myself, in the nobility, beauty, and usefulness of the creatures."

3. (6.) In the Last Days You Shall Have Love, Longing, Fear, and a Threefold Repentance

I asked our Lord how I should act in the last days of my life. He said: "You shall do in your last days as you did in your first. You shall hold yourself in love and longing, repentance and fear, for these four things were the beginning of your life, and they must also be your end." Then I said: "What about the two things that are the foundation and crown of heavenly blessedness, Christian Faith and absolute Trust?" Our Lord said: "Your Faith has become knowledge and your longing has been changed into full assurance." I saw these interpretations in His words and knew them as well in my heart. My threefold repentance lay in three things.

I repent of sin most of all; that comes from love. But I lost the pain of repentance in the fellowship of love. I repent of all human sin. I am like a sick person who longs for things she cannot have. My heart laments over that and my soul chases in its yearning as a hunter after its prey. Our Lord said: "If one cannot capture wild animals any other way, one drives them into the water. If a sinner cannot be converted any other way, she is driven by the prayers of good people into the tears of their hearts."

I am sorrowful for all the good deeds I have needlessly neglected through my love of the flesh. Our Lord said: "One cannot build a house without a site; one cannot receive reward in Heaven without good deeds." But through His heartfelt love, our Lord speaks to each soul: "Take, beloved, this infinite merit you yourself have earned, so God may speak this word in truth to the honor and love of the soul." Therefore, in His love our Lord thinks so tenderly of our works, our poverty, our sufferings we bear in love, that He magnanimously ignores His righteousness. This is the meaning I have grasped from God's multitude of gifts.

4. (9.) *Whoever Honors the Saints is Honored in Return By the Saints, Who Comfort Them in Death*

Because we honor the saints of happy memory with devout intentions on their saint day, they are so joyous that they often appear to us now with all the sovereignty they have won by their merit.

I saw this clearly on the day of St. Mary Magdalene, when we honored God with Hymns of Praise because of the great reward she had received from Him. She floated down into the Choir after the Hymns and looked into the eyes of every singer and said, "All those who honor my end, to their end I will come and honor them in return. According to the grace and merit they have received, so I will honor them." Four great Archangels led her between them and the small angels were too numerous for me to count. I asked what the Archangels were called and she said: "The first is Power, the second Desire, the third Goodwill, the fourth Constancy. With these four virtues I have conquered the sorrow of my heart. Therefore God rewarded me with them. It is similar with other saints." Our Lord said: "If one blows on the tiniest spark it gives heat and light in the Fire of Heaven where the radiant saints abide."

5. (12.) *How You Shall Conduct Yourself in Fourteen Things*

When you pray, make yourself humble.
When you make your confession, be truthful.
When you eat, be moderate.
When you sleep, be modest.

When you are alone, be faithful.
When you are with others, be wise.
When you are taught good habits, follow them.
When your bad habits are reproved, be patient.
When you do evil, seek mercy.
When you are vain, fear yourself.
When you are sad, have great comfort in God.
When you work with your hands, work swiftly.
So you shall drive away evil thoughts.

6. (16.) *How the Soul of Our Lord Dwells in the Holy Trinity and of Its Mission*

When I awake in the night, I reflect on my powers.
Am I, poor creature, worthy to rise and pray for unfaithful Church
That gives my Beloved so much sorrow?
Sometimes He draws me another way, and I am constrained to follow,
Naked, barefoot, and stripped of all earthly things.
Who can urge humanity so gently?
Who can so gently compel the soul?
Who can so highly enlighten the senses
As God who created us and does such mighty things with us?
Thus I thought one night of the Holy Trinity with sweet, effortless flowing of the soul.
Then I saw in the heights the whole blessed Trinity
And the soul of our Lord Jesus Christ.
His soul dwells constant, above all merit, in the Holy Trinity.
There it is embraced and wonderfully wrought,
Shining gloriously above all creaturely beauty
Through the Three Holy Persons.

Then I longed with great humility to speak with our
   Lord's soul in His honor,

For it seemed to me that it performed wondrous works.

Then I soared so near Him, I greeted Him thus:
"Blessed be You, Beloved! What wonders You work in this
everlasting mirror in which all the blessed are so gloriously
seen. You have sweet labor in joyful activity." Then His
soul spoke to unworthy me:

My reflection, You are welcome, for I am a soul as you are

And have carried the burden of all souls in My sinless
   body.

That is My Office.

I ceaselessly move this infinite Godhead and always
   remind the heavenly Father

Of the endless love He bears to human souls.

I also greet My Divine Humanity and thank Him for My
   blessedness

And remind Him how He Himself was an earthly being,

So He may think of the place from which He came.

How great and noble is this human kinship with Him
   that does not allow humanity to be lost.

For no one was conceived or born of his own will,

Therefore you have overcome all your need without sin.

Then I ask the humanity of God to look with special
   compassion so He should see how sick humanity is,

How it was not created without enemies,

But it must ever fight as an armed person whose eyes are
   blindfolded.

Such is the dark nature in which humanity is bound.

Think, noble Son of God, how sorrowful I was on earth
   in You

And stand yet, in fatherly fashion, by all persons who
   bear My likeness, for I am Your soul.

I must urge the Holy Spirit to His task

For He must bring all Heaven's blessedness to the people
of the earth.

Should You then, O God, drive home the bolts of justice

Locking the gates of Heaven so sinners might not enter,

Then I would turn to Jesus Your dear Son

Who through Your mighty power holds in His human
hands the key of Heaven.

That key was forged in the land of the Jews, but when
Jesus turns it

Even the lowliest outcast can enter into the house of
Your Love.

This is the heavenly Father's answer:

My soul cannot endure that I drive sinners from Me.

Thus I pursue many for a long time until I grasp them
firmly and hold them tightly

So none can take them from Me.

Now the Soul of our Lord speaks:

This is My merit, so I am adorned;

My crown is the Godhead,

His humanity is My reward.

The Holy Spirit has enveloped Me and so joyfully penetrated Me

That no creature can resemble or attain Me.

In this Holy Trinity I bear ceaselessly from hour to hour

All earthly sinners, so God may not allow them to fall
into the eternal abyss.

But the Virgin in whom I took refuge as I came out from
the holy Godhead in the humanity of her Son—

She protects all pure souls and laments for the tempted
who repent with fear.

Here before the Holy Trinity the judgment lies in her
hands.

7. (17.) How God Regards Sinners as Converted

Our Lord speaks thus: "It is a fathomless mystery that God can look on sinners as converted people, and that is as it should be. For in order to serve God, people must hasten to Me and not look back; I will carry all burdens borne because of love for Me."

8. (18.) You Shall Examine Your Heart at All Times

Look into your heart at all times with the truth of the Holy Spirit.

Then falsehood will grieve you, for lying drives away Divine love

And confirms in the soul concealed sources of anger and wrath.

9. (19.) Of Good Will Which One Cannot Bring to Good Works

I have suffered much because I could not bring good will to good works.

That made me unstable and powerless, for I did not dare to go against my nature.

For since the time when God let me fall from the heights of bliss down to my own discretion,

I was so bewildered that I could find no end in things,

Seeing that Mighty Love had drawn me here with its flames of fire.

Now, it had flung me into a bottomless pit where I could find no foothold,

Yet that was all I suffered.

I could not call it pain, for I gladly would have been cast out like a mad dog in the very lowest place,

A being without friends, banned, unknown, with poor people in a strange land.

Now, I would not be without obedience,

For holy, humble obedience is the cornerstone of all virtues.

Good will which the good soul has, but which cannot bring it good deeds,

Is like a bright and lovely flower with sweet scent but no fruit.

Then God comforted me:

Good life will pluck eternal joys from good will,

As flowers will weave into the wreaths of His elect, for His eternal marriage,

Those who here were quietly faithful to Him with infinite goodwill, but unable to bring it good works.

Merciful God, stretch out Your Fatherly hand and lead me to the land of Your love.

I have long lost all happiness, and I would willingly win it back with You.

For ease of body and consolation of senses must be received with humble fear,

If one would be in Perfect Truth.

10. (23.) How God Speaks to the Soul in Three States

In the first state the devil often speaks to the soul, but he cannot do so in the other two states. The first state is in the human senses. It is open to God, to devils, and to all creatures to speak to the soul as they please. The second state in which God speaks to the soul is in the soul. Only

God can enter this state. When God speaks in the soul, He does so without the knowledge of the senses and with great, powerful, and swift union between God and the soul. The senses cannot perceive this blissful intercourse. They become so humble that they cannot stand any creature to be more humble than themselves. Shall people humble themselves under the devil? Yes, so much so it may seem to them that their lives have shown contempt to God, because in their daily sins he has often drawn the likeness of the devil on his own soul and has even made deep wounds in it by mortal sins.

The soul caught up into the Holy Spirit cannot stay at such a height. It must always humble itself before all earthly comfort and any delight in such comfort. The soul caught in its own pride leans eagerly toward earthly things.

The third state in which God speaks to the soul is Heaven. He draws the soul up with the generosity of His Will and sets it there to enjoy His wondrous works.

11. (26.) Thoughts of Death and a Long Life are Good

I ponder much and reflect in my human senses how wonderful my soul is. For when I think of death, my soul rejoices so greatly at the thought of leaving this earthly life that my body soars in a supernatural peace beyond words. My senses recognize the marvels that accompany the passing of the soul, so I would most joyfully die at the time God has appointed to me. At the same time, I would gladly live until the last great day and in my heart long for the days of the martyrs that I might have shed blood for the Jesus whom I love. That I dare to say I love God is because a special gift forces me to do so. For when my burdens and sufferings are held before me, my soul begins to burn in the fire of God's true love in such blissful sweetness, that even my body soars in divine bliss. But my senses continue to lament and pray that God would keep from sin all who have injured or maligned me.

12. (28.) When You are About to Die, Take Leave of Ten Things

When I am about to die, I take leave of all from which I must part. I take leave of Holy Church. I thank God I was called to be a Christian and have found real Christian belief. If I were to remain longer here, I would try to help Holy Church, which has many sins.

I take leave of all poor souls now in Purgatory. If I were to remain here longer, I would gladly help expiate their sins. I thank God they will find mercy.

I take leave of all those in Hell and thank God that He exercises His righteousness on them. If I were to remain here longer, I would wish them well.

I take leave of all sinners who lie in mortal sin. I thank God I am not one of them. If I were to remain here longer, I would gladly carry their burden before God.

I take leave of all penitents working out their penance. I thank God I am one of them. If I were to remain here longer, I would always love them.

I take leave of all my enemies. I thank God that they have not conquered me. If I were to remain here longer, I would lay myself under their feet.

I take leave of all earthly things. I am sorrowful before God that I never used them according to His holy ordinances.

I take leave of all my dear friends. I thank God and them that they have been my help in need. If I were to remain here longer, I should always be ashamed of the lack of virtue they must have seen in me.

I take leave of all my wickedness. I am sorrowful before God that I have so greatly spoiled His holy gift to my soul, so that no sin is ever so small that it could be hidden in Heaven. Even though the sin was paid for, the stain remains. I am sorrowful to you, Lord Jesus, for You bear the shame of my sin.

I take leave of my suffering body. I thank God He has preserved me in many things from many sins. Even if I were to remain here longer, the sins of the body are so numerous that I could never be quite free of them.

13. (29.) Of Ten Characteristics of the Divine Fire and of the Nobility of God

An unworthy creature reflected simply upon God's nobility. God showed her in her senses and in the eyes of her soul a Fire that burned ceaselessly in the heights above all things. It had burned without beginning and would burn without end. This Fire is the everlasting God Who has retained in Himself Eternal Life from which all things proceed. The sparks that have blown away from the Fire are the holy angels. The beams of the Fire are God's saints, for their lives cast many lovely lights upon Christianity. The coals of the Fire still glow; they are the just who here burn in heavenly love and enlighten by their good example. The crackling sparks that are reduced to ashes and come to nothing are the bodies of the blessed, who in the grave await their heavenly reward. The Lord of the Fire is still to come, Jesus Christ to whom the Father entrusted the first Redemption and the Last Judgment. On the Last Day He shall make a glorious chalice for the heavenly Father out of the Fire's sparks. On the day of His Eternal Marriage, the Father will drink from this chalice all the holiness that, with His Beloved Son, He has poured into our human souls and our human senses.

The smoke of the Fire is made of all earthly things that people use with wrongful pleasure. They carry much hidden bitterness, no matter how beautiful they are to our eyes or how pleasant they are to our hearts. For they disappear like smoke and blind the eyes of even the highest, until the tears run.

The comfort of the Fire is the joy our souls receive inwardly from God, with such holy warmth from the Divine Fire that we too burn with it and are so sustained by virtues that we are not extinguished. The bitterness of the Fire is the word God shall speak on the Last Day, *Depart from Me, ye cursed, into the everlasting Fire.* The radiance of the Fire is the glowing aspect of the Divine appearance of the Holy Trinity, which so illumines our souls and bodies that we may then see and recognize the marvelous blessedness we cannot even name.

These things have come out of the Fire and flow into it again according to God's laws in everlasting praise:

Do you want to know my meaning?

Lie down in the Fire;

See and taste the Flowing Godhead through your being.

Feel the Holy Spirit moving and compelling you within the Flowing Fire and Light of God.

14. (30.) Pure Love Has Four Things

Pure love of God has these things in it. First, the soul is one with God no matter what happens to it, except for sin. We fervently thank God for this. Second, we must use properly the gifts God has given us in body and soul. Third, we should live purely and in good habits without sin. Fourth, we should practice all virtues. Alas, if only I had them and had them perfected truly in all things. I would have regarded that as the highest contemplation of which I had ever heard. For what good are lofty words without works of mercy? What good is it to love God if we are grim and forbidding to our neighbors? You say, "If God gave me something to do, I would gladly do it." Then listen, the virtues are half a gift from God and half belong to ourselves. When God gives us understanding, we must cultivate and use the virtues.

15. (31.) How God Formed the Soul Out of Blessedness and Suffering; How God Resembles a Cell

I wrote in this book that God is my Father by nature. You do not understand that and say, "All that God has done in us is by Grace and not by nature." You are right and so am I. Listen to this parable: However good a person's eye might be, he cannot see much farther than a mile away. However sharp his senses are, he cannot grasp supernatural things. Except for faith, the person gropes around blindly. Now, the loving soul who loves all God loves and hates all God hates has an eye that God has enlightened. With that eye the soul sees how the Godhead has fashioned our nature in the soul. He has so enfolded the soul in Himself and poured His own Divine nature into it that it can say nothing except that it is by Grace what God is by nature.

The body receives its merit from the Son in brotherly fellowship, as a reward for its labors. The Son of God Himself labored in heartfelt love, poverty, and contempt until His holy death, because of our need. The Holy Spirit also worked His work by His Grace in all the gifts we have ever received. This work is threefold, yet one undivided work God has wrought in us.

Where was God before He created all things? He was in Himself and all things were present and open to Him as they are today. How was our Lord God set there? Everything was enclosed in God as in a cell without a lock or a door. The lower part of the cell is a bottomless prison below every abyss. The upper part is a height above all other heights. The cell's circumference cannot be conceived. God had not yet become the Creator; when He did create all things, the cell was opened up. God is complete in Himself and will ever remain complete. When He became Creator, all creatures became manifest in themselves—humanity, in order to love, enjoy, and know God and be obedient to Him, the animals to know their own nature.

Our knowledge amounts to nothing if we do not love God properly in all things, as He has created all things in orderly love and as He Himself has commanded and taught us.

16. (43.) This Book Flowed From God

The writing of this book flowed out of the living Godhead into Sister Mechthild's heart. It is here truly set down as it flowed into her heart from God and was written down by her own hands. Thanks be to God.

BOOK
VII

1. (3.) How Necessary It Is Always to Look Humbly Into One's Heart

I do not know anyone who is so good that he doesn't need to look ceaselessly into and test and know what is in his heart and also often to find fault with all he does. This must be done with great humility. God's voice taught me this because I never did anything so well that I could not have done it better. My weaknesses thus reproved me: "Wretched creature, how long will you hide your useless habits in your five senses? Our childhood was foolish, our youth troubled. Only God knows how we conquered it. Now in my old age I find much to chide, for it can produce no shining works and is cold and without grace. It is powerless now that it no longer has youth to help it bear God's fiery love. It is also impatient, for now little ills afflict it which in youth it hardly noticed. Yet a good old age is full of patient waiting and trust in God alone."

Seven years ago a troubled old soul lamented these weaknesses to our Lord. God answered: "Your childhood was a companion of My Holy Spirit; your youth was a bride of My humanity; in your old age you are a humble house-wife of My Godhead."

The prayer of the pure heart sometimes awakes sleeping sinners. Alas, poor sinner, how you are to be pitied. You are a self-slayer, a danger to all good. The good person has a great advantage, for when he sees how another sins and falls he looks quickly to himself so he may not so fall. Thus the good person benefits from evil things that good may follow them. But the wicked person becomes more wicked when he sees evil works and examples. He now despises good works and good people. His own perverted wisdom pleases him best.

My good schoolmaster, who taught me how to write this book, also taught me this: Whatever a person does, if he is not genuine, do not trust him. I know an enemy who, if one does not forbid it to enter, destroys God's truth in the heart. If one gives it a chance, it writes false wisdom in the heart that makes it say to itself: "I am by nature weak and bad." But, for that reason you cannot honorably crave God's forgiveness. Through grace you must become strong and good. "But I have no grace." Then with humble tears, steadfast prayer and holy desire, you must ask the God of grace to grant you grace. Thus the worm of evil must die. You must do violence to yourself so that no suffering and no other power can ever gain mastery over you. If we wish to overcome and drive away our anger and all our imperfections, with God's help, then we must secretly stifle our sinful temptations and show ourselves outwardly full of holy joy.

Alas, poor creatures, as long as we storm about in anger, we have no good in us. When we come to ourselves again we must be heartily ashamed of our faults and ashamed that our anger has so undermined our strength and perverted our senses, that the precious time in which we should have served God is lost to us. Alas, what remorse I feel for tears shed in anger and pride, from which the soul becomes so dark that for the time being the creature can do no good thing.

But tears of remorse are so holy that if a sinner would only shed them for all his sins and then remain steadfast, he would never come to everlasting hell. As for the small daily sins a good person has in him and that he will not be able to abandon as long as he lives, if he were to die without confession and penitence, no matter how holy he might be, he must suffer a bitter Purgatory. For, compassionate as God is, He is also just toward sin and anger.

My advice to myself is that we must live humbly, in Love. We shall never become good in darkness. Humility and Love live happily together.

2. (7.) *How Humanity is United to God at All Times*

That humanity is forever united to God is heavenly bliss beyond all earthly joy. How can we attain this? Desire must always accompany all that we do, and if we undertake our work in Christian faith and test it by God's wisdom so that is never useless, then we live with our Lord God in all our works. Thus we are united with Him even in earthly works, through heavenly love. So we will be spiritually enlightened and will praise our Lord God for all the gifts He has ever given us, in our bodies, our friends, our relations—in all the earthly joys we could wish for. If we thank Him for all such earthly gifts, then we are united with Him in sweet love and humble thankfulness.

Thus we should imprint all God's gifts in our hearts: Then our Lord will be full of love. Our senses will be opened and our souls so clear we will see into God's wisdom. We may recognize God's will in all our doings, honor and love Him in sorrowful as well as in joyful gifts, and rejoice in all that happens to us, except sin. We must hate sin. Thus we shall be united already on earth with the saints in Heaven, for God's will is their greatest joy in Heaven.

I do not know how the devil became aware that God had given me this knowledge in the night and that I was thus in union with Him in great joy. The devil came to me and spoke confidentially, for he wished to outwit me. I heard

his voice with my bodily ears and I saw a black, miry creature with my spiritual eyes. Yet, I was not afraid of him, for
when God's gift lives in the soul and wrestles in the senses,
the body cannot fear.

3. (8.) *How Humanity Shall Seek God*

When God sometimes seems to shun humanity, the soul
turns to Him and says, "Lord, my pain is deeper than Hell,
my sorrow is more bitter than the world, my fear greater
than the mountains, my longing higher than the stars. In all
these I cannot find You."

In such distress the soul becomes aware of the presence
of her Love beside her in the guise of a youth of unspeakable beauty. She would have hid, but she fell down at His
feet and kissed His wounds. They were so sweet that she
forgot all her pain and was no longer aware of her old age.
Then she thought, "How gladly you would see His face
even though you must then renounce His wounds. How
gladly would you hear His words and His longing."

Then she stood up clothed in unwavering courage. He
said, "Welcome, beloved!" As He spoke she realized that
every soul whom God serves in His mercy is dear to Him.
He said, "I must protect you from inordinate desire, both
yours and Mine." She said, "My desire for You is unspeakable." Then He said, "Take this crown." The crown He set
on her head shone as if pure gold. This crown of love was
twofold. Then our Lord said, "This crown shall be recognized by all the company of Heaven." She asked, "Will You
receive my soul tomorrow, after I have received Your Holy
Body?" "No," He said, "you will be richer through suffering." "But Lord, what can I do here in this convent?" He
answered, "You shall enlighten and teach and stay here in
great honor." Then she thought, "Now you are here alone

with our Lord." While she was thinking this, she saw two angels beside her, gloriously clothed. Then she said, "How can I now hide myself?" The angels said, "We will accompany you from suffering to suffering, from virtue to virtue, from knowledge to knowledge, from love to Love."

It is hard for me that such a sinful mouth must utter these words, but I dare not refrain, before God. Because of obedience to human frailty and fear of God, I must remember them all my days.

4. (14.) Of God's Choice and Blessing

On another night as I was at my prayers in longing and distress because of my nothingness, I became aware of our Lord. He stood in the Churchyard and had the entire community arranged before Him in order as He entered it. He spoke to them: "I have chosen you. If you choose Me, I will give you something." I asked: "Lord, what will You give them?" He answered: "I will make them bright mirrors on earth so all who see them will recognize the life they live. But in Heaven I will make them radiant mirrors so that all who see them will know I have chosen them." Then He stretched out His hand and blessed them and said: "I bless you with Myself, choose Me in all your thoughts." Those who thus desired Him only were those blessed ones who rightly praised Him. Then I said: "They will ask me how I came to see You." He answered: "There are some among them who know Me."

5. (16.) How Someone Longed and Prayed

There was one who amid the mercies of God and amid much suffering longed continually that God would release her soul in a holy end. Our Lord said: "Await My Will." But the soul said: "Dear Lord, I cannot cease from longing, so glad I would be to be with You." Then our Lord said: "Before the world was, I longed for you; I long for you and you for Me. When two burning desires come together, love is perfected."

6. (19.) A Greeting to Our Lady in the Form of a Litany

I greet you, Lady, Beloved Mary, for you are
> A joy to the Holy Trinity,
> The beginning of all our blessedness,
> The companion of the holy angels here and in God's Kingdom.

I greet you, Lady, Beloved Mary, for you are
A flower of the patriarchs,
> A hope of the prophets,
> A white lily of humble virgins.
> Remember how the salutation of the angel Gabriel came to you.
> Greet my soul on the Last Day and bring me with unclouded joy
> Out of this misery to the happy land of your dear Child
> That there I may find rest.

I greet you, Lady, Beloved Mary, for you are
> A wise teacher of the Apostles,
> A rose of the martyrs,
> A gift of the Confessors,
> A helper of widows,
> An honor of all the saints of your dear Child.
> Pray for me that I, unworthy though I am, may be sanctified in everything I do,
> Mary, Beloved Queen.

I greet you, Lady, Beloved Mary, for you are
>A refuge for sinners,
>A strong helper for the perplexed,
>A comforter to Holy Church,
>A dread to evil spirits,
>Who are driven away before you.
>Drive them far from me that they may never delight
>>themselves in me
>But that I may ever be constant in your service.

7. (20.) *How We Should Offer a Hail Mary to Our Lady*

Greetings, Queen of Heaven, Mother of God, and our beloved Lady! Receive a Hail Mary this day to the praise and glory of that wonderful moment when Father, Son, and Holy Spirit looked joyfully into the young face of the Virgin Mother, frank, open, and full of blessedness.

>Lady, I think of that in all my longings, all my prayers,
>All my sufferings, all my need, all my heart's sorrow
>>and the honor
>Of my soul at the latter end.
>When I make my way from this sad world,
>That must all be offered ceaselessly to your motherly
>>care, your maidenly honor, and your joyful goodness.
>I add all who with me are your friends and mine
>In the name of Almighty God,
>Mary Beloved, Queen of Heaven.

8. (21.) How the Heart Shall be Examined Before Going to the Table of the Lord

You ask me to teach when I am myself unlearned. What you desire you will find a thousandfold in your books.

When I, a poor sinner, go to receive the Body of the Lord, I examine my soul in the mirror of my sins. There I see truly how I have lived, how I am now living, and how I am going to live. In this mirror I see nothing but woe and remorse. Then I cast my eyes on the ground and lament and weep, for the Eternal, Incomprehensible God is so good that He will even bend down to enter the muddy pool of my heart. Then I reflect that it is just that my body should be dragged to the gallows as a thief who has stolen from her rightful master the precious treasure of Clearness that God gave me in holy baptism:

That we must sadly lament all the days of our life,
Since we have so often darkened the clearness You gave us.
Father, we beg Your forgiveness.
If a sinner does not confess sin and turns against confession,
She shall not receive the Body of the Lord.
But now I go on in Hope, thanking my God who made me
That I might receive the Body of Christ.
Now I go to the Table rejoicing to receive the slain Lamb
Who chose to endure the Cross, five times wounded and torn.
It is well for us that these things happened.
I, so unworthy, weep when I behold His holy sorrows.
Make your souls a cradle and lay the Beloved there
With joyful and loving hearts,

Offering Him praise and glory,
The One who endured a bed with the cattle.
Therefore we bow before Him.
Sense and spirit say
Lord! Beloved! I thank You,
Give me Your treasure so I may dwell in Your innocence.
Where then, Lord, shall I rest You?
All my soul is Your house:
Enter, enter in!
It is a house of sorrow that I had forgotten,
Remembering only Your woe.
Rest then upon my sorrow, my coverlet of longing,
Lay Your head on my grief.
I have been too proud, now forgive me,
Now I accept Your pain.
Now I renounce my pride and ask You a favor,
Asking You for my soul's joy to give me those sinners
    who lie over there in mortal sin.
Now my sorrow and Yours have rested in peace together.
Now is our love made whole.
Guest, raised from the dead, keep me close to You in
    consolation and bliss.
What more can our love say,
Now that You dwell in the house of my sorrow?
Risen for the dead You come in to me;
Comfort me, my Beloved, and hold me in Your presence
    in continual joy.
Allow me to pay the price of those sinners in Purgatory.
The price must not hurt Another.
Now, Lord, in Your ascending, having given Yourself to
    me, spare me not too much.
In all ways I must die for love, that is all I desire.
Give me and take from me what You will.
But leave me this—to die of love in loving!

9. (25.) Of the Greeting of the Holy Trinity

Though I am poor in virtue,
Though I am small in spiritual stature,
May I venture to greet those heights of crystal, bliss,
    nobility, wisdom,
Uniting the Trinity?
All things that are or shall be flow from those cloudless
    heights;
I must enter always anew into that flood.
But how?
I must kneel, for I am guilty,
I must struggle, being idle,
I must run, for diligence fails me.
I must fly and soar in all things beyond myself,
But then, when I am wearied, return to the flood again.
What my welcome is now, the eyes have not seen and
    the ears have not heard:
Glory to you, Trinity!

10. (26.) How One Should Flee to God in Temptation

Lord Jesus Christ, I, poor creature, flee You but long for
    Your help,
For my enemies pursue me.
Lord God, I implore You, for they would separate me
    from You.
Do not give me into their power, but keep me pure in
    You.
You who have redeemed me by Your death, be now my
    help and comfort.
Let me not fall into destruction, You who willed to die
    for me.

Lord Jesus Christ, I seek Your help.
Wake my soul from the sleep of indolence,
Enlighten my senses from the darkness of my flesh,
Give me Your guidance and direct my ways to You with-
out sin,
So far as it is possible to humanity.
For Your eyes see all my deficiencies.
Holy Mary, Mother of God, Queen of Heaven,
Be my helper, for I am guilty;
Help me to find mercy in Your dear Child.
Mother of all purity, I pour forth all my sorrows to you.
Hail, Queen!

11. (27.) How a Spiritual Person Should Turn Her Heart from the World

When a spiritual person sees her dearest friends and relations richly adorned according to the ways of the world,
then she must be armed by the Holy Spirit lest she should
think the world is also mighty. Because on that thought her
heart will become so dark and her senses so unprepared for
God and her spirit so lax toward prayer and her soul so outcast, that she will inwardly resemble her worldly friends
more than a spiritual person:

If she would stand well with God,
There must be a struggle,
And her conscience, which is still a lantern of the Holy
Spirit, will be troubled.
For the conscience is lit no longer if it lacks the light of
the Spirit.
If that light has burnt out in the lantern, the beauty of
the lantern can no more be seen.
Thus it is with a spiritual person
To whom all worldly display is as horror in her heart.

Yet if she keeps her lantern filled, its light will not go out.

But if her heart stands open to the world, then is her lantern broken.

For the bitter north wind of greed blows from our friends and relations

Who lament our need and poverty

While they sink in the muddy pool of the world and are drowned in their sins.

Then our light is extinguished and yet we have not the world.

Then comes the south wind of false delight in the world that seems so beautiful

But yet has so much bitter pain;

If this should please us, we walk to our everlasting hurt.

Of that we must beware, for there is no sin so small that it is not an eternal blot on our souls.

No sin that it was better never to have committed was ever changed into holiness.

Therefore if we would stand well with God, we must stand prayerfully before Him in fear.

For that which we have given Him we can never take back again without hurting ourselves.

The fish looks eagerly at the red fly with which the fisherman will catch him,

But it does not see the hook.

So it is with the poison of the world; its danger is not realized.

If you will truly turn away from it, look at Your Bridegroom.

Lord of all worlds, He stands there gloriously robed in priestly robes, blood red, ebony black,

Scourged, bound to a pillar, where through love for you He received many sharp wounds.

Let the wounds gladly enter your heart and you will
    gladly forego the lure of the world.
If you would follow Him with holy thoughts, look up:
See how He hung on the Cross lifted up on high for all
    the world to see His body flecked with blood.
This garment of His shall be the treasure of Your heart,
His kingly eyes ever flowing with tears, his sweet heart
    pierced with love.
Now hear the voice that teaches you God's love:
How the hammers of the smiths drove in the nails
    through His hands and feet on the Cross.
Think too of the wound of the spear that pierced His
    side to the heart, and tell Him all your sins
So you will come to know God.
See the sharp crown of thorns He wore on His head,
And seek to earn His Grace.
He will give you enough of all blessedness.
Thank Him that He willed to die through His great love
    for you
And let no one deceive you,
So you may be a Queen in His Kingdom for ever:
If you should attain this, you will overcome with joy
All the sorrows of the world.

12. (32.) How the Works of Good People Shine Beside the Works of Our Lord

See in the following how the works of good people shall
glow and shine in heavenly glory:
    Insofar as we have been innocent here, so far will God's
        holiness shine in our innocence.
    Insofar as we do good works here, so far will the works of

God shine and glow in our works.

Insofar as we here cling with fervor to God, so far will God's fervor multiply and shine through ours.

Insofar as we here thankfully accept our sufferings and bear them patiently, so far will God's sufferings enlighten and shine through our sufferings.

Insofar as we have diligently practiced the virtues here, so far will God's holy virtues light and shine in ours in infinite honor.

Insofar as we here burn with love and radiate the light of a holy life, so far will God's love burn in and illumine our souls and bodies without ceasing, never to be extinguished.

These reflections shine and radiate from the eternal Godhead.

These good works we have received from God's holy humanity,

And brought to pass through the power of the Holy Spirit.

Thus all our lives and works flow back again into the Holy Trinity:

There we shall see clearly how we stand with God here.

Insofar as we live here in God's love,

So far shall we soar in bliss in the heavenly heights,

So far will the power of love be given us in reward,

That we may be able to use all our wills in action.

But in order to be recognized by the saints there as we have been here,

We must have been their friends.

13. (33.) Of Spiritual Drink

I am ill and I long deeply for the health-giving drink which Jesus Christ Himself drank

When as God and man He came to the Manger.

The drink was ready for Him there, and He drank of it
   so deeply that He was on fire with love
And instilled His heart's sorrow into all the virtues.
He always gave virtue, and His goodness never failed.
This health-giving drink pleases me, the drink of suffer-
   ing-for-the-love-of-God.
Suffering is bitter, so we add an herb to it—Glad-suffering,
   and a second called Patience-in-suffering.
These too are bitter and so we add another herb, Holy
   Fervor, that makes Patience sweet.
It helps us wait long in suffering, for everlasting life and
   our salvation.
But waiting is too bitter and we add another herb,
   Unwearied Joy!
Dear Lord, if You would but give me this drink, I should
   live unwearied with Joy in suffering.
Then I would give up for a time the joys of Heaven,
   much as I long for them.
Now You, Lord, of Your dear will, must give this drink to
   me and all who ask for it through Your Love.

14. (34.) Of Spiritual Food

After the bitter drink, a light diet is necessary. Aspiring
desire, deepening humility, and overflowing love are like
three virgins who lead the soul up to God in Heaven. There
it sees its Love and says, "Lord, I grieve that You are troubled
by those dearest to You on earth, the Christians. I grieve that
Your friends are so greatly hindered by Your enemies."

Our Lord said: "Those who have real goodness in them
turn everything that happens to them to the Glory of God,
except sin. Therefore suffering claims first place. It is of
first importance that when people are not comforted by
God's will, He remains patient. That would not be so if

people were comforted according to their own will, for God's Will is clear and perfect, while human will is grievously tangled with the flesh. All who inwardly love fervently, become outwardly still, for outward activity hinders the inward working of the spirit. What the spirit then sings inwardly sounds far sweeter than any earthly song."

Patience sings most sweetly of all, more sweetly than even the angelic choirs, for since the angels feel no suffering, they can have no patience. This we have through our Lord's humanity, as well as the honor by which God honors us on earth and to which we shall be exalted in Heaven. Through the noble works of our Lord and His holy sufferings, our Christian works and our willing suffering are made noble and sanctified because our dear Lord was baptized in them.

Lord, so help us that our holy striving may never rest and our deepening humility may never raise itself up through pride, but instead the flowing, burning love of God may here be our Purgatory, in which all our sins may be washed away.

15. (37.) Of the Everlasting Marriage of the Holy Trinity

Whoever will prepare herself in true love for the heavenly marriage of the Holy Trinity
Must always begin thus:
She must follow and serve the heavenly Father without ceasing, in holy fear
And deep humility in all things.
She must follow and serve the Son in patient suffering and willing poverty in holy works.
She must follow and serve the Holy Spirit in holy hope, beyond all words,
With a pure and gentle heart, that her goodness may be felt.

The loving virgins shall follow the Son of the pure Virgin,

The noble Youth Jesus Christ who is still as full of love as He was when He was eighteen years old.

Therefore is He most to be loved,

"Fairer than the children of men" to the virgins who follow Him

With tender delight in the flowery meadow of their pure conscience.

There He plucks for them the flowers of all the virtues that they weave into noble wreaths

To be carried at the everlasting marriage.

After the noble rites have taken place at which Christ Himself will serve,

A great Dance of Praise begins at which each body and soul wears the wreath of the virtues

They have perfected here with much holy prayer.

Thus they follow the Lamb in unspeakable bliss,

From bliss to love, from love to joy, from joy to clearness, clearness to power,

From power to the highest heights before the eyes of the heavenly Father.

Then He greets His only-begotten Son as well as many pure brides who have come with Him:

"Beloved Son, what You are, that I am, and what they are delights Me."

Rejoice evermore, beloved brides,

Rejoice in My everlasting clearness and lament only softly of pain and sorrow.

My holy angels shall serve you,

My saints shall honor you,

The mother of My Son's humanity shall receive you, her companions, with praise.

Rejoice, beloved brides!

My Son shall embrace you, and My Godhead shall

permeate you,

My Holy Spirit shall lead you ever further in blissful
delight according to your will.

What more could you want?

I Myself will love you!

Those who are not virgins may witness this marriage and
take part in it as far as they can.

I heard and saw all this with my soul's eyes in one short
hour. Then I became again the speck of dust and ashes I
had always been.

16. (38.) How a Spiritual Person Shall Lament and Acknowledge Her Sins to God Every Day

I, a sinful creature, lament and acknowledge to God

All the sins of which I am guilty in His sight, and all the
good works I have neglected.

I acknowledge and lament all the sins I committed
before I knew what sin was,

And I lament the sins I committed knowingly with
anger, idleness, and vanity.

Lord, have mercy upon me, for I am truly sorry for them,

And give me Your full assurance that You have forgiven
me all,

Otherwise, I could no longer live in joy, Jesus, My
Beloved.

Let me come to You in true remorse and heartfelt love

And let my love never grow cold,

But let me feel Your love in my heart, my soul, my senses,
and all my members;

Then my love can never grow cold.

17. (40.) The Loving Soul Speaks to Her Lord

If all the world were mine and if it were pure gold
And I could by desire always stay here as the noblest,
    loveliest, richest Queen,
All that would be worthless to me!
I would much rather see Christ my beloved Lord in
    heavenly glory.
Alas, what they who have to wait long for His coming
    suffer.

18. (42.) Of the Honey Drink

Lord God, close now Your treasured gift by a holy end—
Raise it up so it may be a praise to You in Heaven and earth.
Then a voice said,
"You shall receive from Me a honey drink which comes
    from many woods
And I will make it free so others may also enjoy it."

19. (43.) Of Love's Simplicity

Those who would know much but love little remain
    always at the beginning of a good life.
Therefore we should always carry awe in our hearts if we
    want inwardly to please God.
For simple love, even with little knowledge, works great
    things within.
Holy simplicity is the way to all wisdom:
    It shows the wise they are nothing but fools,
For when simplicity of heart lives in the wisdom of the
    senses,
Much holiness comes to the human soul.

20. (46.) How the Soul Offers Itself in Spiritual Poverty

Here the soul offers itself to go forth to God in spiritual poverty, everlasting love, and longing. It speaks thus: The long waiting is forgotten; in the future it seems possible that God and the soul may be united, never to be separated. When I think of that my heart is full of Joy!

Dear Lord, how still is now Your silence.

I thank You evermore that You have shunned me so long,

You must evermore be praised so Your will, not mine, be done.

Now I hold fast to Your own words that I have heard in Christian teaching:

"Whoever loves Me I will love, and My Father will love him and we will come unto him

And make our abode in him."

How blessed I am, dear Lord, because of Your merciful goodness.

You will never go back on Your word.

Then our Lord spoke:

"When your waiting is over and I come to fetch you and give you heavenly gifts,

I will come swiftly, for My Eternity awaits you.

I will unfold it and will raise the soul from the bleeding earth,

For nothing could be dearer to Me."

God's eternal love dwells in the soul, passing love of earthly things dwells in the flesh

And the five senses have the power to choose to which they will turn.

21. (55.) A Friend Writes to a Friend

Because you love God above your human might and with all the power of your soul; because you acknowledge Him with all the wisdom of your soul; because you have received His gifts with great and holy thankfulness, I write you this letter.

The overflow of Divine Love that ceaselessly and tirelessly pours forth is so great that our little vessel is filled to the brim and overflows. If we do not choke the channel with self-will, God's gifts continue to flow and overflow.

Lord, You are full and You fill us with Your gifts. You are great and we are small. How shall we become like You? Lord, You have given us so much, and we must also give to others. Even though we are a small vessel, You have filled us. A small vessel can be emptied into a larger one until it becomes too full. The larger vessel is the plenitude of grace that God receives from our works. We are so small that a little word of God or of Holy Scripture completely fills us and we can hold no more. Then we empty this gift into the large vessel that is God. How can we do this? We must pour out what we have received with holy desire on sinners, so they may be cleansed. But now the vessel is full again. Therefore we pour it out on the imperfections of spiritual people so they might fight more boldly and become and remain more perfect. Again the little vessel is filled. Again we pour it out, on the needs of the poor souls who suffer in Purgatory, so God in His Mercy may release them from their infinite need. Or else we sprinkle with Divine compassion the needs of Holy Church, for she lies in many sins. God loved us from the beginning; He has labored for us from the beginning and has suffered greatly for us. If we want to be like Him, we must give it all back to Him.

Our Lord thus spoke to a certain person: "Give Me all

that is yours, and I will give you all that is Mine." This exchange of love we give God is sweet indeed. The exchange of work is very burdensome for us, for that which love has inwardly enjoyed, the creature must sometimes learn to do without outwardly. If one asks how difficult that is, I could never explain with human understanding. Our Lord suffered much for us, and even died for us. But a little pain of ours seems to be very great. I despise this in myself and lament before God that I have so few virtues. Love makes suffering sweeter than words can express, and if we want to be like God, we must win many battles. The thoughts of God and of the loving soul mingle as air is infused by sunshine. In that sweet union the sun melts the frost and overcomes the darkness so imperceptibly we cannot recognize it as the same sun. Thus it is with Divine Love. May God give us and keep us all in this Love. Amen.

22. (56.) How God Touches His Friends With Suffering

When people have sorrow the cause of which they do not know
And yet are aware of little sins,
Our Lord says to them,
"I have touched you in the same way in which My Father let Me be touched on earth.
In those whom I there draw to Myself,
That causes much suffering.
But my friends should know truly that the more I draw them the nearer they come to Me.
When people conquer the self, so that suffering and consolation weigh equally,
Then I will raise them to blessedness and let them taste Eternal Life."

23. (64.) How God Serves Humanity; A Prayer

Thus speaks a beggar woman in her prayer to God:

Lord, I thank You that since in Your love You have taken from me all earthly riches, You now clothe and feed me through the goodness of others, so that I no longer know those things that might clothe my heart in pride of possession.

Lord, I thank You that since You have taken my sight from me, You serve me through the eyes of others.

Lord, I thank You that since You have taken from me the strength of my hands and the strength of my heart, You now serve me with the hands and hearts of others.

Lord, I pray for them. Reward them here on earth with Your Divine Love so they may faithfully serve and please You with all virtues until they come to a happy end.

I pray for all those with pure hearts who gave up all for love of God.

They are all archbeggars and will be judged by Jesus our Redeemer on the Last Day.

Lord, all that I lament before You I pray You will change in me and in all sinners.

All that I ask I pray You to grant to me and all imperfect spiritual people for Your own glory.

Lord, Your praise shall never be silent in my heart, whatever I do or leave undone or suffer. Amen.